Vocal Expression

by Katherine Jewell Everts

PLAN OF THE BOOK

HOW TO SUPPORT THE TONE. Directions and Exercises.

HOW TO FREE THE TONE. Directions and Exercises.

HOW TO RE-ENFORCE THE TONE. Directions and Exercises.

TO THE PUPIL

Let me trace the evolution which has led to the plan of this text-book. A class in elocution of which you are a member is given a paragraph from Modern Eloquence, a bit from an oration or address of Beecher or Phillips or Beveridge, to study. The passage appeals to you. You are roused by it to an eager, new appreciation of courage, conservatism or of the character of some national hero. You "look" your interest. You are asked to go to the platform. You are glad. You want to repeat the inspired word of the prophet. You begin confidently to voice the words of the great orator--the words which you had lifted alive from the page--but in your voice they sound now formal, cold, lifeless. You hesitate, your emotion is killed, your thought inhibited, your eagerness gone, your impulse dead--but you have made a discovery. You have become conscious of a great need, and your teacher, if she be wise, has discovered the nature of that need. You consult together and find three things have failed you, and, through you, the orator you wished to interpret. These things are your mind, your vocabulary, and your voice. You find that your need is threefold--it is the need to feel intelligently and to think vitally on your feet; the need to acquire a vocal vocabulary; the need to train your instruments of expression--voice and body.

To help you and your teacher to meet this threefold need is the wish of this book; and the book's plan is the result of the author's experience with her own pupils in watching the evolution of their skill in vocal expression, the development, along natural lines, of their ability to speak effectively.

VOCAL EXPRESSION

INTRODUCTION

The strongest impulse of the human heart is for self-expression. The simplest form of expression is speech. Speech is the instinctive use of a natural instrument, the voice. The failure to deal justly with this simple and natural means of expression is one of the serious failures of our educational system. Whether the student is to wait on another's table or be host at his own; whether he is to sell "goods" from one side of a counter or buy them from the other; whether he is to enter one of the three great professions of law, medicine, or theology; "go on the stage" or platform; become Minister to France or President of the United States, it remains precisely true that to speak effectively will be essential to his success, and should be as essential to his own happiness as it will be to that of all involved in his pursuit of success.

Yet, if we give heed at all to the question of voice and speech, it is our last, not our first, consideration. We still look upon the mind as a storehouse instead of a clearing-house. We continue to concern ourselves with its ability to take in, not its capacity to give out. Voice and speech are still left to shift for themselves during the period of school life when they should be guarded and guided as a most essential equipment for life after school days are over. To convert the resultant hard, high-pitched, nasal tone which betrays the American voice into the adequate agent of a temperament which distinguishes the American personality, and to help English speech in this country to become an efficient medium of lucid intercourse, such is the object of this book.

In an address upon the "Question of Our Speech" delivered before a graduating class at Bryn Mawr, several years ago, Mr. Henry James said:

"No civilized body of men and women has ever left so vital an interest to run wild, to shift, as we say, all for itself, to stumble and flounder, through mere adventure and accident, in the common dust of life, to pick up a living, in fine, by the wayside and the ditch.

"The French, the Germans, the Italians, the English, perhaps, in particular, and many other people, Occidental and Oriental, I surmise, not excluding the Turks and the Chinese, have for the symbol of education, of civility, a tone-standard; we alone flourish in undisturbed and in something like sublime unconsciousness of any such possibility."

So searching an arraignment by so eminent a scholar before an audience of so high a degree of intelligence and culture seems to have been necessary to command an adequate appreciation of the condition of "Our Speech" and to incite an adequate effort toward reform. Since the arraignment was made and afterward published, classes have been organized, books written, and lectures delivered in increasing abundance, forming a veritable speech crusade--and the books and the classes and the lectures have availed much, but the real and only "reliable remedy" lies with the teacher in the public and private schools and colleges of the United States. And it is to the teacher of English and Elocution that this Class Book on Vocal Expression is offered.

Learning to Talk might have been a truer, as it had been a simpler, title, yet the more comprehensive phrase has justifiable significance, and we have chosen it in the same spirit which discards for the text-book in Rhetoric or English Composition the inviting title Learning to Write.

There is a close analogy between the evolution of vocal and the evolution of verbal expression. The method of instruction in the study of the less heeded subject of the "Spoken Word" throws an interesting light on the teaching of the more regarded question of the "Written Word." An experience as teacher of expression and English in a normal school in Minnesota has influenced the author of these pages to so large an extent in the formulation of her own method of study, and so in the plan of this volume, that it seems advisable to record it. To the work of reading or expression to which she was originally called two classes in composition were added. The former teacher of composition had bequeathed to the work as a text-book a rhetoric which consisted of involved theory plus one hundred and twenty-five separate and distinct rules for the use of words, and the teacher of expression found, to her amazed dismay, that the students had been required to learn these rules, not only "by heart," but by number, referring to them as rule six or thirty-six or one hundred and twenty-five, according to the demanded application.

A week, possibly a fortnight, passed in silent struggle, then the distracted teacher of expression went to the president of the school with these questions: "Of what avail are one hundred and twenty-five rules for the use of words when these children have less than that number of words to use, and no desire to acquire more? Could you make teachers of these normal students by giving a hundred and more laws for the governing of pupils and the imparting of the material of knowledge, if you furnished neither pupils nor material upon which to test the laws?" "Certainly not!" was the restful reply of one of the wisest of the educators I have known. "May I lay aside the text-book and read with these students in English for a little?" "You may teach them to write English in any way you can!"

The next day the class in composition was discovered eagerly reading Tennyson's Holy Grail, stopping to note this felicitous phrase, that happy choice of words, the pertinent personnel of a sentence or paragraph. The first examination of the term consisted in a series of single questions, written on separate slips of paper and laid face down on the teacher's desk. Each student took one of these slips which read, "Tell in your own words the story of The Coming of Arthur, the Holy Grail, Lancelot and Elaine or Guinevere," as the chance of the chooser might allot a given idyl. The experiment was a success. The president was satisfied with the papers in English composition. Each student had had "something to say" and had said it. Each student had words at his command little dreamed of in his vocabulary before the meeting with the Knights of the Round Table.

The first step toward a mastery of Verbal Expression had been successfully taken! The consciousness of need--the need of a vocabulary--had been awakened. The desire to supply that need--to acquire a vocabulary--had been aroused. A way to acquire a vocabulary had been made manifest. Out of such consciousness alone is born the willingness to work upon which progress in the mastery of any art depends. To the teacher of expression it seemed no more advisable now than it had seemed before, to ask the students to learn either "by heart" or by number the one hundred and twenty-five rules of technique. But the great laws governing the use of a vocabulary she now found her students eager to study, to understand, and to apply. She found her class willing to enter upon the drudgery which a mastery of technique in any art demands.

So in the teaching of Vocal Expression, he who begins with rules for the use of this change of pitch or that inflection, this pause or that color of tone, before he has aroused in the pupil the desire to express a vivid thought, and so made him conscious of the need to command subtle changes of pitch, swift contrasts in tone and turns of inflection, will find himself responsible for mechanical results sadly divorced from true and natural speech. But let the teacher of expression begin, not with rules of technique, but with the material for inspiration and interpretation; let him rouse in the pupil the impulse to express and then furnish the material and means for study which shall enrich the vocabulary of expression and he will find the instruments of the art--voice and speech--growing into the free and efficient agents of personality they are intended by nature to be.

* * * * *

In March, 1906, the editor of Harper's Bazar began a crusade in the interest of the American voice and speech. Through the issues of more than a year the magazine published arraignment, admonition, and advice on this subject. It was the privilege of the author of this volume to contribute the last four articles in that series. In response to a definite demand from the readers of the Bazar these articles were later embodied in a little book called The Speaking Voice. In a preface to this book the author confesses her "deliberate effort to simplify and condense the principles fundamental to all recognized systems of vocal instruction," making them available for those too occupied to enter upon the more exhaustive study set forth in more elaborate treatises. The book was not intended for hours of class-room work in schools or colleges, but for the spare moments of a business or social life, and its reception in that world was gratifying. But, to the author's delight, the interest aroused created a demand in the schools and colleges for a real text-book, a book which could be put into the hands of students in the departments of English and expression in public and private institutions and colleges, and especially in normal schools. It is in response to that appeal that this class-book in Vocal Expression is issued; and it is to the teachers whose impelling interest and enthusiasm in the subject justify the publication of this volume that the author desires first to express her grateful appreciation.

To Miss Frances Nash, of the Lincoln High School in Cleveland, for her invaluable advice in determining the exact nature of the need which the book must meet, and for her assistance in choosing the material for interpretation, my gratitude and appreciation are especially due.

To others whose influence through books or personal instruction has made this task possible, acknowledgment made in The Speaking Voice is reiterated.

PART I

STUDIES IN VOCAL INTERPRETATION

PRELIMINARY STUDY

TO ESTABLISH A CONSCIOUS PURPOSE

"The orator must have something in his very soul he feels to be worth saying. He must have in his nature that kindly sympathy that connects him with his fellow-men and which so makes him a part of the audience that his smile is their smile, his tear is their tear, the throb of his heart the throb of the hearts of the whole assembly."--HENRY WARD BEECHER.

We have said that whatever part in the world's life we choose or are chosen to take, it remains precisely true that to speak effectively is essential to fulfilling, in the highest sense, that function. Whether the occupation upon which we enter be distinguished by the title of cash-girl or counsellor at law; dish-washer or d 閣 utante; stable-boy or statesman; artist in the least or the highest of art's capacities, crises will arise in that calling which demand a command of effective speech. The situation may call for a slow, quietly searching interrogation or a swift, ringing command. The need may be for a use of that expressive vocal form which requires, to be efficient, the rugged or the gracious elements of your vocabulary; the vital or the velvet tone; the straight inflection or the circumflex; the salient or the slight change of pitch; the long or the short pause. Whatever form the demand takes, the need remains for command of the efficient elements of tone and speech if we are to become masters of the situation and to attain success in our calling. How to acquire this mastery is our problem. How to take the first step toward acquiring that command is the subject of this first study.

Is there a student reader of these pages who has not already faced a situation requiring for its mastery such command? Listen to Mr. James again:

"All life, therefore, comes back to the question of our speech, the medium through which we communicate with each other; for all life comes back to the question of our relations with each other. These relations are possible, are registered, are verily constituted by our speech, and are successful in proportion as our speech is worthy of its human and social function; is developed, delicate, flexible, rich--an adequate accomplished fact. The more we live by it, the more it promotes and enhances life. Its quality, its authenticity, its security, are hence supremely important for the general multifold opportunity, for the dignity and integrity, of our existence."

Is there one among you whose relations with others would not have been rendered simpler, truer, clearer at some critical moment had your "speech been more worthy of its great human and social function?" Then, do you hesitate to enter upon a study which shall make for clarified relations and a new "dignity and integrity of existence?" Anticipating your reply, I invite you to take a first step in Vocal Expression. How shall we approach the subject? How did you begin to master any one of the activities in which you are more or less proficient? How did you learn to swim, or skate, or play the violin? Not by standing on the shore and gazing at the water or ice! Not by looking at violins in shop windows! No! You began by leaping into the water, putting on your skates and going out on the ice; taking the violin into your hands and drawing the bow across the strings. But you say: "We have taken the step which corresponds to these in speech! We can talk!" Exactly! But what command of the art of skating or swimming or playing the violin would the artist in any of these activities have achieved had he been content to stop with the act of jumping into the water, going out on the ice, or drawing the bow across the violin? The question's answer calls up an illuminating analogy. Are not most of us in regard to our mastery of speech in the condition of the skater, the swimmer, the fiddler in the first stage of those expressive acts? Are we not floundering in the water, fallen on the ice, or alienating the ears of our friends? "We are so! We confess it!"--every time we speak.

And so to-day we shall offer no argument against entering upon an introductory study--we shall take our first step in the Art of Vocal Expression. But we shall take it in a new spirit--the spirit of an artist bent upon the mastery of his art. If we flounder or fall, we shall not be more content in our ignominy than is the choking swimmer or the prostrate skater. If we produce painful instead of pleasing sounds with our instrument, we shall not persist in a merciless process of tone production; but we shall proceed to study diligently the laws governing the control of the instrument until we have mastered its technique and made it an agent of harmonious intercourse. We shall take the first steps with a conscious purpose, the purpose to make our speech worthy of its great social and human function.

Then in this spirit I invite you "to plunge." I furnish as the material for your experiment these sentences:

DISCUSSION OF DIRECT APPEAL

Do you ask me, then, what is this Puritan principle?

The Puritan principle in its essence is simply individual freedom!--CURTIS.

Mind your own business with your absolute will and soul, but see that it is a good business first.--RUSKIN.

Back to the bridge and show your teeth again, Back to the bridge and show to God your eyes!--MACKAYE.

What news, and quickly!--MACKAYE.

Do not pray for tasks equal to your powers. Pray for powers equal to your tasks.--PHILLIPS BROOKS.

Hence! home, you idle creatures, get you home. Is this a holiday?--SHAKESPEARE.

And so, gentlemen, at this hour we are not Republicans, we are not Democrats, we are Americans!--CURTIS.

I shall not discuss the interpretation of these sentences with you. I shall not interpret them for you. Such discussion and interpretation is your part in this study. But you are not to discuss them with a pencil on paper; you are to interpret them with your voice to another mind.

Let us stop here and consider together for a few moments this act which we call Vocal Interpretation (which might be more simply designated as Reading Aloud), and with which these first studies are concerned. What does it mean to vocally interpret a piece of literature--a poem, a play, a bit of prose; a paragraph, a sentence, or even a single word? It means that you, the interpreter, must transfer the thought contained in that word, phrase, sentence, or paragraph from the printed page to the mind of an auditor. It means that you must take the thought out of the safety vault and put it into circulation. That is your problem, and it presents three factors. You cannot slight any one of these factors and expect to successfully solve your problem. These factors are: your author's thought, your own voice, and your auditor's mind.

We shall concern ourselves in this first study with the last of these three factors--the mind of the auditor, or, to put it more definitely, your attitude toward the mind of your auditor. We shall make this our first concern, not because it is more essential to successful delivery than the other two elements of the problem, but because failure at this point is a fundamental failure. Such failure involves the whole structure in ruin.

Let me make this point explicit. Failure of the speaker to direct the thought toward a receiving mind--the mind of an auditor--results in blurred thought, robs the voice of all aim, and reduces the interpretation to a meaningless recital of words. Consider the first factor in the problem of interpretation--the thought of the author. Take these first two sentences:

Do you ask me, then, what is this Puritan principle?

The Puritan principle in its essence is simply individual freedom!

A wholly satisfying interpretation of these lines involves a knowledge of the speech from which they are taken, and a knowledge of the circumstances under which it was delivered. Complete possession of the thought, which alone insures perfect expression, requires a grasp of the situation out of which it was born and an appreciation of the mind which conceived it. But with no context and no knowledge of these conditions, and so only an approximate appreciation of the thought in all its fulness, the interpreter, under the stimulus of an intent to convince another of the truth contained in the detached sentence, may deliver the lines convincingly! And to carry conviction is the first and fundamental requisite of all good delivery.

So it is with the second factor in your problem. Your voice may fail at a dozen different points, but directed thought can employ so skilfully even an inefficient instrument that the resultant expression, while never satisfying, may still carry conviction.

But let the one who speaks these lines feel no responsibility toward another, let him fail to direct the idea toward another mind, and the most complete possession of the author's thought, plus the most perfect control of the voice, will fail to make the interpretation convincing. You must establish a relation with your auditor! You must have an aim. You must "have something to say," but you must also have some one "to say it at." You cannot hope to become an expert marksman by "shooting into the air."

Then once more I bid you approach the subject of Vocal Interpretation in a new spirit. Let your study of the thought in these sentences hold in its initial impulse this idea: "I have something I must tell you!" Try prefacing your interpretation with some such phrase as this: "Listen to me!" or, "I want to tell you something."

I would suggest as a preliminary exercise that you should try "shooting at a mark" these single words: "No!" "Yes!" "Come!" "Go!" "Aim!" "Fire!" "Help!" "What ho!"

Listen to me!

"You will find the gayest castles in the air far better for comfort and for use than the dungeons that are daily dug and caverned out by grumbling, discontented people."--EMERSON.

Let me tell you something!

"Might is right, say many, and so it is. Might is the right to bear the burdens of the weak, to cheer the faint, to uplift the fallen, to pour from one's own full store to the need of the famishing."--NAPIER.

It is the angel-aim and standard in an act that consecrates it. He who aims for perfection in a trifle is trying to do that trifle holily. The trier wears the halo, and, therefore, the halo grows as quickly round the brows of peasant as of king.--GANNETT.

Think twice before you speak, my son; and it will do no harm if you keep on thinking while you speak.--ANONYMOUS.

Sweet friends Man's love ascends, To finer and diviner ends Than man's mere thought e'er comprehends.

--LANIER.

SUGGESTIVE ANALYSIS

HAMLET'S SPEECH TO THE PLAYERS

Hamlet: Speak the speech, I pray you, as I pronounced it to you, trippingly on the tongue: but if you mouth it, as many of your players do, I had as lief the town-crier spoke my lines. Nor do not saw the air too much with your hand, thus; but use all gently: for in the very torrent, tempest, and, as I may say, whirlwind of your passion, you must acquire and beget a temperance that may give it smoothness....

Be not too tame, neither, but let your own discretion be your tutor: suit the action to the word, the word to the action; with this special observance, that you o'erstep not the modesty of nature, for anything so overdone is from the purpose of playing, whose end, both at the first and now, was and is, to hold, as 'twere, the mirror up to nature; to show virtue her own feature, scorn her own image, and the very age and body of the time his form and pressure.

--SHAKESPEARE.

Let us consider together the problem of vocally interpreting this speech of Hamlet's, keeping the mind of the auditor constantly before us, the special factor in our problem which is the concern of this study. What is the first point to be determined? The situation, is it not? Remember, in our previous discussion I have made it clear that it is not essential to our present purpose that we should know, in determining our situation, the exact conditions under which this speech was delivered. Neither is it essential to our present purpose that we should make an exhaustive study of the play of "Hamlet" or of the character of the Prince of Denmark. Lest you mistake me I must reiterate the fact that an interpretation of these lines, looked upon as Hamlet's speech, would require just such exhaustive study of context and character--study which would lead to that complete possession which alone insures perfect expression; but it is legitimate at this point in our study of vocal expression to use this text quite apart from its context as a perfect example of direct appeal. It is legitimate to imagine a situation of our own in which this thought could be pertinently expressed. We must then first determine what you, the speaker, are to represent, and the nature of the audience you are to address. One word in the text more than any other, perhaps, determines these points--the word "players." With this word as a key to a probable situation, let us imagine that you, the one who must "speak this speech," are a stage-director of your own play, and that we, the class to whom you must speak, are a company of players (actors, as we now call them) which is about to present your play. The fact that this is exactly the situation in Shakespeare's play from which this speech is taken is interesting, but does not affect our attitude toward the text. But that we should assume the state of mind which animated the author of the Mouse-trap, is vital to our problem. Hamlet was intent upon getting an effect incalculably potent from the delivery of the "speech" he "had pronounced." You must imagine that you have written not merely a play, but a play which you intend shall have a powerful influence upon the lives of the people who are to hear it. Once more, then, let us determine the exact situation. You, the author of a moving play--you, its stage-director--have called us, your actors, together for rehearsal. You know just how you wish the lines of your play delivered. It is absolutely vital to the success of your venture that we, the actors, should grasp your ideal of delivery and act upon it. You must convince us that this is the only way in which you will permit the text to be handled. You are the orator as Mr. Beecher has drawn him for us. You will realize, in thinking your way through this appeal, that, while the stage-director is addressing the whole company of players, he has singled out from the others one who is to deliver a particular speech from his play. It is well to follow this idea of the situation. Include us all, then, as a class in your chosen cast, but single out one of us, and speak directly at the mind of that one. Look him straight in the eye. Direct your thought in the main to his mind, even while your thought reaches out and draws us all into the circle of its enthusiasm. Now, with this attitude and intent toward an audience, try to vocally interpret, to think aloud this thought. What is the trouble? "Speak the speech" you say, "is a difficult combination of words to utter"? "'Trippingly' trips up your tongue"? "You don't understand the reference to a 'town-crier'"?

Ah, what discoveries we are making!

"You feel that you should be able to illustrate your own ideal of delivery by delivering these directions after the very manner you ask your players to observe"? That might legitimately be expected of you, I think. "But this you cannot do!" What a shocking confession! Yes, but how good to have this new knowledge of your own ability, or, in this case, disability. How appalling to find that you cannot easily utter the simple combination of words, "Speak the speech, I pray you," without stumbling; that any word, a plain, simple English word, trips your tongue. How appalling, but how encouraging it is! For the discovery of this fact, the consciousness of these limitations, "constitutes half the battle" before us. It is a battle. But you shall be equipped to meet it. Turn to the chapters on "Freeing the Tone." Find the exercises for training the tongue. Faithful practice of these exercises (even without direction, but, if you are a member of the class in expression for which this book was made, under direction) will very shortly conquer the unruly tongue for use in uttering any difficult combination of words. And your teacher will patiently "pick you up" (in this first study) every time you trip over a word or phrase, and she will patiently refer you to the corner of history which will explain any unfamiliar portions of your text if you will persistently try to do your part at this point. That part is, to think the thought before you directly at another's mind. That is all we ask at this point. Make this direct appeal for simplicity in delivery straight to the mind of him whom you have chosen to receive, and act upon it. Talk to me if I am your chosen player! Convince me! Make me realize what you expect of me! Make me want to meet your expectation! Make me afraid to fail you!

With these suggestions and this direct appeal to you, I leave you with your teacher and with the following material chosen for your preliminary study in Vocal Interpretation.

SELECTIONS FOR INTERPRETATION

There was once a noble ship full of eager passengers, straining at full speed from England to America. Two-thirds of a prosperous voyage thus far were over, and in our mess we were beginning to talk of home.

Suddenly a dense fog came, shrouding the horizon, but, as this was a common occurrence in the latitude we were sailing, it was hardly mentioned in our talk. A happier company never sailed upon an autumn sea. When a quick cry from the lookout, a rush of officers and men, and we were grinding on a ledge of rocks off Cape Race. I heard the cry, "Every one on deck!" and knew what that meant--the masts were in danger of falling. A hundred pallid faces were huddled together near the stern of the ship where we were told to go and wait.

Suddenly we heard a voice up in the fog in the direction of the wheel-house ringing like a clarion above the roar of the waves. As the orders came distinctly and deliberately through the captain's trumpet to "Shift the cargo," to "Back her," to "Keep her steady," we felt, somehow, that the commander up there in the thick mist knew what he was about.

When, after weary days of anxious suspense, the vessel leaking badly, we arrived safely in Halifax, old Mr. Cunard, agent of the line, on hearing from the mail officer that the steamer had struck on the rocks and been saved by the captain's presence of mind and courage, replied, simply: "Just what I might have expected. Captain Harrison is always master of the situation."

No man ever became master of the situation by accident or indolence. "He happened to succeed" is a foolish, unmeaning phrase. No man happens to succeed. "What do you mix your paints with?" asked a visitor of Opie, the painter. "With brains, sir," was the artist's reply. *??

There are men who fail of mastery in the world from too low an estimate of human nature. "Despise nothing, my son," was the advice a mother gave to her boy when he went forth into the untried world to seek his fortune, and that boy grew up into Sir Walter Scott. *??

In case of great emergency it took a certain general in our army several days to get his personal baggage ready. Sheridan rode into Winchester without even a change of stockings in his saddle-bags. *??

All great leaders have been inspired with a great belief. In nine cases out of ten, failure is borne of unbelief.--Masters of the Situation, JAMES T. FIELDS.

Once more unto the breach, dear friends, once more; Or close the wall up with our English dead! In peace, there's nothing so becomes a man As modest stillness and humility; But when the blast of war blows in our ears, Then imitate the action of the tiger: Stiffen the sinews, summon up the blood, Disguise fair nature with hard-favoured rage: *?? Hold hard the breath, and bend up every spirit To his full height! On, on, you noblest English, Whose blood is fet from fathers of war-proof! Fathers that, like so many Alexanders, Have in these parts from morn till even fought, And sheathed their swords for lack of argument. *?? I see you stand like greyhounds in the slips, Straining upon the start. The game's afoot: Follow your spirit; and, upon this charge Cry--God for Harry! England! and St. George!--Henry V., SHAKESPEARE

Fourscore and seven years ago our fathers brought forth, on this continent, a new nation, conceived in liberty, and dedicated to the proposition that all men are created equal. Now we are engaged in a great civil war, testing whether that nation, or any nation so conceived and so dedicated, can long endure. We are met on a great battlefield of that war. We have come to dedicate a portion of that field, as a final resting-place for those who here gave their lives that that nation might live. It is altogether fitting and proper that we should do this.

But, in a larger sense, we cannot dedicate--we cannot consecrate--we cannot hallow--this ground. The brave men, living and dead, who struggled here have consecrated it, far above our power to add or detract. The world will little note nor long remember what we say here, but it can never forget what they did here. It is for us, the living, rather, to be dedicated here to the unfinished work which they who fought here have thus far so nobly advanced. It is rather for us to be here dedicated to the great task remaining before us-- that from these honored dead we take increased devotion to that cause for which they gave the last full measure of devotion--that we here highly resolve that these dead shall not have died in vain--that this nation, under God, shall have a new birth of freedom--and that government of the people, by the people, for the people, shall not perish from the earth.--Address at Gettysburg, ABRAHAM LINCOLN.

From an address delivered in the Auditorium, at Chicago, on the afternoon of February 22, 1902, on the occasion of the celebration of Washington's Birthday.

The meaning of Washington in American history is discipline. The message of Washington's life to the American people is discipline. The need of American character is discipline.

Washington did not give patriotism to the American colonies. The people had that as abundantly as he. He did not give them courage. That quality was and is in the American blood. He did not even give them resource. There were intellects more productive than his. But Washington gave balance and direction to elemental forces. He was the genius of order. He was poise personified. He was the spirit of discipline. He was the first Great Conservative. It was this quality in him that made all other elements of the Revolution effective. It was this that organized our nebulous independence into a nation of liberty. The parts of a machine are useless until assembled and fitted each to its appropriate place. Washington was the master mechanic of our nation; so it is that we are a people.

But we are not yet a perfect people. We are still in the making. It is a glorious circumstance. Youth is the noblest of God's gifts. The youth of a nation is like the youth of a man. The American people are young? Yes! Vital? Yes! Powerful? Yes! Disciplined? Not entirely. Moderate? Not yet, but growing in that grace. And therefore on this, his day, I bear you the message of Washington--he, whose sanity, orderliness, and calm have reached through the century, steadying us, overcoming in us the untamed passions of riotous youth.--Conservatism; the Spirit of National Self-Restraint, ALBERT BEVERIDGE.

We have noted in our introduction the close analogy which exists between the evolution of vocal expression and the evolution of verbal expression. Let us not fail to follow this analogy through the various studies which make up this one study of interpretation. We have begun our work in vocal expression with the subject of direct appeal. What corresponds to this step in the evolution of verbal expression?

Mr. J. H. Gardiner, in his illuminating text for the student of English composition, called The Forms of Prose Literature,[1] discusses these forms first under the two great heads of the "Literature of Thought" and the "Literature of Feeling," and then under the four sub-titles which all instruction in rhetoric recognizes as the accepted divisions of literature: Exposition, Argument, Description, and Narrative. We do not find the exact parallel for our study in direct appeal under these subheads. Do we? No. In order "to take the plunge" in the study of English composition which shall correspond to our preliminary effort in interpretation, we must set aside for the moment the question of exposition, to be entered upon as a "first study" in verbal expression corresponding to the question of vitality in thinking, which is our first study in vocal expression, and look for a parallel "preliminary study" in composition.

[1] The Forms of Prose Literature, courtesy of Messrs. Charles Scribner's Sons.

In his comparative study of exposition and argumentation Mr. Gardiner says: "An exceedingly good explanation may leave its reader quite unmoved: a good argument never does. Even if it does not convert him, it should at least make him uncomfortable. Now, when we say that argument must move its reader, we begin to pass from the realm of pure thought, in which exposition takes rise, to that of feeling, for feeling is a necessary preliminary to action. How large a part feelings play in argument you can see if you have ever heard the speech of a demagogue to an excited crowd. It is simply a crass appeal to their lower passions, aided by all the devices of oratory, often, perhaps, also by a moving presence. A better example is Henry Ward Beecher's Liverpool speech, in which he won a hearing from a hostile mob by an appeal to their sense of fair play. Such cases show how far argument may get from the simple appeal to the understanding, how little it may be confined to the element of thought. The prime quality, therefore, of argument is persuasiveness."

Not argument, then, but the element in argument, called persuasion, furnishes the study in composition which corresponds to direct appeal in interpretation. And just as truly as your intent to convince another mind of the truth of your author's thought will often take care of all other elements in the problem of its vocal expression and result in convincing interpretation, so the intent to persuade another mind of the truth of your own thought will often take care of all other elements in the problem of verbal expression and result in moving composition.

Following Mr. Gardiner a little further in his discussion of persuasion, we find our study in interpretation in direct accord with his advice in the study of composition, for he says: "This element of persuasion belongs to that aspect of literature which has to do with the feelings; and, as depending on the personal equation of the writer, it is much less easy than the intellectual element to catch and generalize from, and almost impossible to teach. All that I can do is to examine it in good examples, and then make very tentatively a few suggestions based on these examples. For it cannot too often be written down in such a treatise as this that the teacher of writing can no more make a great writer than the teacher of painting can turn out a new Rembrandt or a Millet; in either case the most that the teacher can do is to furnish honest and illuminating criticism, and to save his pupil unnecessary and tedious steps by showing him the methods and devices which have been worked out by the masters of the craft."

In treating the question of pure style, as another division of the power of persuasion, Mr. Gardiner says: "It is almost impossible to give practical help toward acquiring this gift of an expressive style; the ear for the rhythm and assonance of style is like an ear for music, though more common, perhaps. It is good practice to read aloud the writing of men who are famous for the quality, and, when you read to yourself, always to have in mind the sound of what you read. The more you can give yourself of this exercise, the more when you write, yourself, will you hear the way your own style sounds."

With our idea for a combined study of the two great forms of expression reinforced by such authority, let us, in taking our next step in this preliminary study in vocal expression, make it also a preliminary study in verbal expression by using as our next selection for interpretation, not a fragment of an address or a part of an oration, but a complete example of persuasive discourse. Such an example we find in this sermon of Mr. Gannett's "Blessed be Drudgery." And, as we try our growing powers of lucid interpretation upon this subject-matter, let us stop to note its verbal construction and its obedience to the laws of persuasive discourse. The interpretation must be made in the class-room, because interpretation needs an immediate audience; the analysis of the literary form may be made in your study: the two processes should be carried on as far as possible together.

BLESSED BE DRUDGERY[2]

[2] This sermon is published with the kind permission of the author and the publisher.

I

Of every two men probably one man thinks he is a drudge, and every second woman is sure she is. Either we are not doing the thing we would like to do in life; or, in what we do and like, we find so much to dislike that the rut tires even when the road runs on the whole, a pleasant way. I am going to speak of the Culture that comes through this very drudgery.

"Culture through my drudgery!" some one is now thinking: "This treadmill that has worn me out, this grind I hate, this plod that, as long ago as I remember it, seemed tiresome--to this have I owed 'culture'? Keeping house or keeping accounts, tending babies, teaching primary school, weighing sugar and salt at a counter, those blue overalls in the machine shop--have these anything to do with 'culture'? Culture takes leisure, elegance, wide margins of time, a pocket-book; drudgery means limitations, coarseness, crowded hours, chronic worry, old clothes, black hands, headaches. Culture implies college: life allows a daily paper, a monthly magazine, the circulating library, and two gift-books at Christmas. Our real and our ideal are not twins--never were! I want the books,--but the clothes-basket wants me. The two children are good,--and so would be two hours a day without the children. I crave an outdoor life,--and walk down-town of mornings to perch on a high stool till supper-time. I love Nature,--and figures are my fate. My taste is books,--and I farm it. My taste is art,--and I correct exercises. My taste is science,--and I measure tape. I am young and like stir,--the business jogs on like a stage-coach. Or I am not young, I am getting gray over my ears, and like to sit down and be still,--but the drive of the business keeps both tired arms stretched out full length. I hate this overbidding and this underselling, this spry, unceasing competition, and would willingly give up a quarter of my profits to have two hours of my daylight to myself,--at least I would if, working just as I do, I did not barely get the children bread and clothes. I did not choose my calling, but was dropped into it--by my innocent conceit, or by duty to the family, or by a parent's foolish pride, or by our hasty marriage; or a mere accident wedged me into it. Would I could have my life over again! Then, whatever I should be, at least I would not be what I am to-day!"

Have I spoken truly for any one here? I know I have. Goes not the grumble thus within the silent breast of many a person, whose pluck never lets it escape to words like these, save now and then on a tired evening to husband or to wife?

There is often truth and justice in the grumble. Truth and justice both. Still, when the question rises through the grumble, Can it be that drudgery, not to be escaped, gives "culture"? the true answer is--Yes, and culture of the prime elements of life; of the very fundamentals of all fine manhood and fine womanhood.

Our prime elements are due to our drudgery--I mean that literally; the fundamentals that underlie all fineness and without which no other culture worth the winning is even possible. These, for instance--and what names are more familiar? Power of attention; power of industry; promptitude in beginning work; method and accuracy and despatch in doing work; perseverance; courage before difficulties; cheer under straining burdens; self-control and self-denial and temperance. These are the prime qualities; these the fundamentals. We have heard these names before! When we were small mother had a way of harping on them, and father joined in emphatically, and the minister used to refer to them in church. And this was what our first employer meant--only his way of putting the matter was, "Look sharp, my boy!"--"Be on time, John!"--"Stick to it!" Yes, that is just what they all meant: these are the very qualities which the mothers tried to tuck into us when they tucked us into bed, the very qualities which the ministers pack into their platitudes, and which the nations pack into their proverbs. And that goes to show that they are the fundamentals. Reading, writing, and arithmetic are very handy, but these fundamentals of a man are handier to have; worth more; worth more than Latin and Greek and French and German and music and art-history and painting and wax flowers and travels in Europe added together. These last are the decorations of a man or woman: even reading and writing are but conveniences: those other things are the indispensables. They make one's sit-fast strength and one's active momentum, whatsoever and wheresoever the lot in life be--be it wealth or poverty, city or country, library or workshop. Those qualities make the solid substance of one's self.

And the question I would ask of myself and you is, How do we get them? How do they become ours? High-school and college can give much, but these are never on their programmes. All the book processes that we go to the schools for, and commonly call "our education," give no more than opportunity to win these indispensables of education. How, then, do we get them? We get them somewhat as the fields and valleys get their grace. Whence is it that the lines of river and meadow and hill and lake and shore conspire to-day to make the landscape beautiful? Only by long chiselings and steady pressures. Only by ages of glacier crush and grind, by scour of floods, by centuries of storm and sun. These rounded the hills, and scooped the valley-curves, and mellowed the soil for meadow-grace. There was little grace in the operation, had we been there to watch. It was "drudgery" all over the land. Mother Nature was down on her knees doing her early scrubbing work! That was yesterday: to-day, result of scrubbing-work, we have the laughing landscape.

Now what is true of the earth is true of each man and woman on the earth. Father and mother and the ancestors before them have done much to bequeath those elemental qualities to us; but that which scrubs them into us, the clinch which makes them actually ours, and keeps them ours, and adds to them as the years go by--that depends on our own plod, our plod in the rut, our drill of habit; in one word, depends upon our "drudgery." It is because we have to go, and go, morning after morning, through rain, through shine, through toothache, headache, heartache, to the appointed spot, and do the appointed work; because, and only because, we have to stick to that work through the eight or ten hours, long after rest would be so sweet; because the school-boy's lesson must be learned at nine o'clock and learned without a slip; because the accounts on the ledger must square to a cent; because the goods must tally exactly with the invoice; because good temper must be kept with children, customers, neighbors, not seven, but seventy times seven times; because the besetting sin must be watched to-day, to-morrow, and the next day; in short, without much matter what our work be, whether this or that, it is because, and only because, of the rut, plod, grind, humdrum in the work, that we at last get those self-foundations laid of which I spoke,-- attention, promptness, accuracy, firmness, patience, self-denial, and the rest. When I think over that list and seriously ask myself three questions, I have to answer each with No:--Are there any qualities in the list which I can afford to spare, to go without, as mere show-qualities? Not one. Can I get these self-foundations laid, save by the weight, year in, year out, of the steady pressures? No, there is no other way. Is there a single one in the list which I cannot get in some degree by undergoing the steady drills and pressures? No, not one. Then beyond all books, beyond all class-work at the school, beyond all special opportunities of what I call my "education," it is this drill and pressure of my daily task that is my great school-master. My daily task, whatever it be--that is what mainly educates me. All other culture is mere luxury compared with what that gives. That gives the indispensables. Yet fool that I am, this pressure of my daily task is the very thing that I so growl at as my "drudgery"!

We can add right here this fact, and practically it is a very important fact to girls and boys as ambitious as they ought to be,---the higher our ideals, the more we need those foundation habits strong. The street-cleaner can better afford to drink and laze than he who would make good shoes; and to make good shoes takes less force of character and brain than to make cures in the sick-room, or laws in the legislature, or children in the nursery. The man who makes the head of a pin or the split of a pen all day long, and the man who must put fresh thought into his work at every stroke,--which of the two more needs the self-control, the method, the accuracy, the power of attention and concentration? Do you sigh for books and leisure and wealth? It takes more "concentration" to use books--head tools--well than to use hand tools. It takes more "self-control" to use leisure well than workdays. Compare the Sundays and Mondays of your city; which day, all things considered, stands for the city's higher life,--the day on which so many men are lolling, or the day on which all toil? It takes more knowledge, more integrity, more justice, to handle riches well than to bear the healthy pinch of the just-enough.

Do you think that the great and famous escape drudgery? The native power and temperament, the outfit and capital at birth, counts for much, but it convicts us common minds of huge mistake to hear the uniform testimony of the more successful geniuses about their genius. "Genius is patience," said who? Sir Isaac Newton. "The Prime Minister's secret is patience," said who? Mr. Pitt, the great Prime Minister of England. Who, think you, wrote, "My imagination would never have served me as it has, but for the habit of commonplace, humble, patient, daily, toiling, drudging attention"? It was Charles Dickens. Who said "The secret of a Wall Street million is common honesty"? Vanderbilt; and he added as the recipe for a million (I know somebody would like to learn it), "Never use what is not your own, never buy what you cannot pay for, never sell what you haven't got." How simple great men's rules are! How easy it is to be a great man! Order, diligence, patience, honesty,--just what you and I must use in order to put our dollar in the savings-bank, to do our school-boy sum, to keep the farm thrifty, and the house clean, and the babies neat. Order, diligence, patience, honesty! There is wide difference between men, but truly it lies less in some special gift or opportunity granted to one and withheld from another, than in the differing degree in which these common elements of human power are owned and used. Not how much talent have I, but how much will to use the talent that I have, is the main question. Not how much do I know, but how much do I do with what I know? To do their great work the great ones need more of the very same habits which the little ones need to do their smaller work. Goethe, Spencer, Agassiz, Jesus, share, not achievements, but conditions of achievement, with you and me. And those conditions for them, as for us, are largely the plod, the drill, the long disciplines of toil. If we ask such men their secret, they will uniformly tell us so.

Since we lay the firm substrata of ourselves in this way, then, and only in this way; and since the higher we aim, the more, and not the less, we need these firm substrata,--since this is so, I think we ought to make up our minds and our mouths to sing a hallelujah unto Drudgery: Blessed be Drudgery,--the one thing that we cannot spare!

II

But there is something else to be said. Among the people who are drudges there are some who have given up their dreams of what, when younger, they used to talk or think about as their "ideals"; and have grown at last, if not content, resigned to do the actual work before them. Yes, here it is,--before us, and behind us, and on all sides of us; we cannot change it; we have accepted it. Still, we have not given up one dream,--the dream of success in this work to which we are so clamped. If we cannot win the well-beloved one, then success with the ill-beloved,--this at least is left to hope for. Success may make it well-beloved, too,--who knows? Well, the secret of this success still lies in the same old word, "drudgery." For drudgery is the doing of one thing, one thing, one thing, long after it ceases to be amusing; and it is this "one thing I do" that gathers me together from my chaos, that concentrates me from possibilities to powers, and turns powers into achievements. "One thing I do," said Paul, and, apart from what his one thing was, in that phrase he gave the watchword of salvation. That whole long string of habits--attention, method, patience, self-control, and the others--can be rolled up and balled, as it were, in the word "concentration." We will halt a moment at the word:

"I give you the end of a golden string: Only wind it into a ball,-- It will lead you in at Heaven's gate, Built in Jerusalem's wall."

Men may be divided into two classes,--those who have a "one thing," and those who have no "one thing," to do; those with aim, and those without aim, in their lives: and practically it turns out that almost all of the success, and, therefore, the greater part of the happiness, go to the first class. The aim in life is what the backbone is in the body: without it we are invertebrate, belong to some lower order of being not yet man. No wonder that the great question, therefore, with a young man is, What am I to be? and that the future looks rather gloomy until the life-path opens. The lot of many a girl, especially of many a girl with a rich father, is a tragedy of aimlessness. Social standards, and her lack of true ideals and of real education, have condemned her to be frittered: from twelve years old she is a cripple to be pitied, and by thirty she comes to know it. With the brothers the blame is more their own. The boys we used to play our school games with have found their places; they are winning homes and influence and money, their natures are growing strong and shapely, and their days are filling with the happy sense of accomplishment,--while we do not yet know what we are. We have no meaning on the earth. Lose us, and the earth has lost nothing; no niche is empty, no force has ceased to play, for we have got no aim, and therefore we are still--nobody. Get your meaning first of all! Ask the question until it is answered past question, What am I? What do I stand for? What name do I bear in the register of forces? In our national cemeteries there are rows on rows of unknown bodies of our soldiers,--men who did a work and put a meaning to their lives; for the mother and the townsmen say, "He died in the war." But the men and women whose lives are aimless reverse their fates. Our bodies are known, and answer in this world to such or such a name,--but as to our inner selves, with real and awful meaning our walking bodies might be labeled, "An unknown man sleeps here!"

Now, since it is concentration that prevents this tragedy of failure, and since this concentration always involves drudgery, long, hard, abundant, we have to own again, I think, that that is even more than what I called it first,--our chief school-master; besides that, drudgery is the gray Angel of Success. The main secret of any success we may hope to rejoice in is in that angel's keeping. Look at the leaders in the profession, the "solid" men in business, the master-workmen who begin as poor boys and end by building a town in which to house their factory hands; they are drudges of the single aim. The man of science, and to-day more than ever, if he would add to the world's knowledge, or even get a reputation, must be, in some one branch at least, a plodding specialist. The great inventors, Palissy at his pots, Goodyear at his rubber, Elias Howe at his sewing-machine, tell the secret,--"One thing I do." The reformer's secret is the same. A one-eyed, grim-jawed folk the reformers are apt to be: one-eyed, grim-jawed, seeing but the one thing, never letting go, they have to be, to start a torpid nation. All these men as doers of the single thing drudge their way to their success. Even so must we, would we win ours. The foot-loose man is not the enviable man. A wise man will be his own necessity and bind himself to a task, if by early wealth or foolish parents or other lowering circumstances he has lost the help of an outward necessity.

Again, then, I say, Let us sing a hallelujah and make a fresh beatitude: Blessed be Drudgery! It is the one thing we cannot spare.

III

This is a hard gospel, is it not? But now there is a pleasanter word to briefly say. To lay the firm foundations in ourselves, or even to win success in life, we must be drudges. But we can be artists, also, in our daily task. And at that word things brighten.

"Artists," I say,--not artisans. "The difference?" This: the artist is he who strives to perfect his work,--the artisan strives to get through it. The artist would fain finish, too; but with him it is to "finish the work God has given me to do!" It is not how great a thing we do, but how well we do the thing we have to, that puts us in the noble brotherhood of artists. My Real is not my Ideal,--is that my complaint? One thing, at least, is in my power: if I cannot realize my Ideal, I can at least idealize my Real. How? By trying to be perfect in it. If I am but a rain-drop in a shower, I will be, at least, a perfect drop; if but a leaf in a whole June, I will be, at least, a perfect leaf. This poor "one thing I do,"--instead of repining at its lowness or its hardness, I will make it glorious by my supreme loyalty to its demand.

An artist himself shall speak. It was Michael Angelo who said: "Nothing makes the soul so pure, so religious, as the endeavor to create something perfect; for God is perfection, and whoever strives for it strives for something that is godlike. True painting is only an image of God's perfection,--a shadow of the pencil with which he paints, a melody, a striving after harmony." The great masters in music, the great masters in all that we call artistry, would echo Michael Angelo in this; he speaks the artist essence out. But what holds good upon their grand scale and with those whose names are known, holds equally good of all pursuits and all lives. That true painting is an image of God's perfection must be true, if he says so; but no more true of painting than of shoemaking, of Michael Angelo than of John Pounds, the cobbler. I asked a cobbler once how long it took to become a good shoemaker; he answered, promptly, "Six years,--and then you must travel!" That cobbler had the artist soul. I told a friend the story, and he asked his cobbler the same question: How long does it take to become a good shoemaker? "All your life, sir." That was still better,--a Michael Angelo of shoes! Mr. Maydole, the hammer-maker, of central New York, was an artist: "Yes," said he to Mr. Parton, "I have made hammers here for twenty-eight years." "Well, then, you ought to be able to make a pretty good hammer by this time." "No, sir," was the answer, "I never made a pretty good hammer. I make the best hammer made in the United States." Daniel Morell, once president of the Cambria Railworks in Pittsburgh, which employed seven thousand men, was an artist, and trained artists. "What is the secret of such a development of business as this?" asked the visitor. "We have no secret," was the answer; "we always try to beat our last batch of rails. That's all the secret we have, and we don't care who knows it." The Paris bookbinder was an artist, who, when the rare volume of Corneille, discovered in a book-stall, was brought to him, and he was asked how long it would take him to bind it, answered, "Oh, sir, you must give me a year, at least; this needs all my care." Our Ben Franklin showed the artist when he began his own epitaph, "Benjamin Franklin, printer." And Professor Agassiz, when he told the interviewer that he had "no time to make money"; and when he began his will, "I, Louis Agassiz, teacher."

In one of Murillo's pictures in the Louvre he shows us the interior of a convent kitchen; but doing the work there are, not mortals in old dresses, but beautiful white-winged angels. One serenely puts the kettle on the fire to boil, and one is lifting up a pail of water with heavenly grace, and one is at the kitchen dresser reaching up for plates; and I believe there is a little cherub running about and getting in the way, trying to help. What the old monkish legend that it represented is, I hardly know. But, as the painter puts it to you on his canvas, all are so busy, and working with such a will, and so refining the work as they do it, that somehow you forget that pans are pans and pots pots, and only think of the angels, and how very natural and beautiful kitchen-work is,--just what the angels would do, of course.

It is the angel-aim and standard in an act that consecrates it. He who aims for perfectness in a trifle is trying to do that trifle holily. The trier wears the halo, and therefore, the halo grows as quickly round the brows of peasant as of king. This aspiration to do perfectly,--is it not religion practicalized? If we use the name of God, is this not God's presence becoming actor in us? No need, then, of being "great" to share that aspiration and that presence. The smallest roadside pool has its water from heaven, and its gleam from the sun, and can hold the stars in its bosom, as well as the great ocean. Even so the humblest man or woman can live splendidly! That is the royal truth that we need to believe,--you and I who have no "mission," and no great sphere to move in. The universe is not quite complete without my work well done. Have you ever read George Eliot's poem called "Stradivarius"? Stradivarius was the famous old violin-maker, whose violins, nearly two centuries old, are almost worth their weight in gold to-day. Says Stradivarius in the poem:

"If my hand slacked, I should rob God,--since He is the fullest good,-- Leaving a blank instead of violins. He could not make Antonio Stradivari's violins Without Antonio."

That is just as true of us as of our greatest brothers. What, stand with slackened hands and fallen heart before the littleness of your service! Too little, is it, to be perfect in it? Would you, then, if you were Master, risk a greater treasure in the hands of such a man? Oh, there is no man, no woman, so small that they cannot make their life great by high endeavor; no sick crippled child on its bed that cannot fill a niche of service that way in the world. This is the beginning of all gospels,--that the kingdom of heaven is at hand just where we are. It is just as near us as our work is, for the gate of heaven for each soul lies in the endeavor to do that work perfectly.

But to bend this talk back to the word with which we started: will this striving for perfection in the little thing give "culture"? Have you ever watched such striving in operation? Have you never met humble men and women who read little, who knew little, yet who had a certain fascination as of fineness lurking about them? Know them, and you are likely to find them persons who have put so much thought and honesty and conscientious trying into their common work--it may be sweeping rooms, or planing boards, or painting walls--have put their ideals so long, so constantly, so lovingly into that common work of theirs, that finally these qualities have come to permeate not their work only, but so much of their being that they are fine-fibred within, even if on the outside the rough bark clings. Without being schooled, they are apt to instinctively detect a sham,--one test of culture. Without haunting the drawing-rooms, they are likely to have manners of quaint grace and graciousness,--another test of culture. Without the singing-lessons, their tones are apt to be gentle,--another test of culture. Without knowing anything about Art, so called, they know and love the best in one thing,--are artists in their own little specialty of work. They make good company, these men and women,--why? Because, not having been able to realize their Ideal, they have idealized their Real, and thus in the depths of their nature have won true "culture."

You know all beatitudes are based on something hard to do or to be. "Blessed are the meek": is it easy to be meek? "Blessed are the pure in heart": is that so very easy? "Blessed are they who mourn." "Blessed are they who hunger and thirst--who starve--after righteousness." So this new beatitude by its hardness only falls into line with all the rest. A third time and heartily I say it,--"Blessed be Drudgery!" For thrice it blesses us: it gives us the fundamental qualities of manhood and womanhood; it gives us success in the thing we have to do; and it makes us, if we choose, artists,--artists within, whatever our outward work may be. Blessed be Drudgery,--the secret of all culture!

And now, as a final step in this preliminary study, a step which shall again give practice in both forms of expression, you are to choose from your vital interests one concerning which you hold intense convictions. First you are to set forth these convictions in the strongest piece of persuasive prose you can command: this is work for your study. Second, you are to summon all your vocal resources, and, with the one idea of persuading us of the truth of your convictions, make to us for them a direct appeal: this work is for the class-room. So shall we have combined the preliminary study in vocal expression of direct appeal with the preliminary study in verbal expression of persuasion.

FIRST STUDY

TO ESTABLISH VITALITY IN THINKING

Among the axioms of our subject-matter already formulated stands this one:

reading aloud is thinking aloud. If reading aloud is thinking aloud the quality of the reading will depend, of course, upon the quality of the thinking. But while clear thinking does not assure lucid reading (since there are other elements in the problem), the converse is true, that good reading implies clear thinking. For it is impossible to read convincingly unless one is thinking vitally, which brings us to the object of this study: To Establish Vitality in Thinking.

Do you know what it means to think vitally in reading? It means a concentration of your mind upon the thought before you until you, yourself, seem to be thinking that thought for the first time,--until you seem to be bringing forth a thought of your own conception instead of rethinking the conception of another's mind. Is this a familiar experience? It must become one if you are to become a true interpreter. For the true interpreter is first of all the keen thinker.

We do not say of the great actor, after a performance of Hamlet, "He played Hamlet wonderfully!" We say, rather, "He was Hamlet." The great actor creates the part he plays each time he plays it. He creates the part by living the part. Even in the same way the great interpreter creates the thought he voices through a concentration of mind which appropriates the thought and makes it his own to voice.

We have said that the greatest need of the human heart is for self-expression. To satisfy the heart that act of expression must be a creative act. True interpretation is creative expression. The fundamental step toward creative expression is complete possession of the thought to be expressed. Complete possession depends upon your power to concentrate your mind upon a thought until it is your own. The first step in interpretation is to establish vitality in thinking.

The new arithmetic trains the mind to see the relation behind the mathematical statement of the relation. The child who "says his tables" to-day is not repeating by rote words and figures, he is realizing vital relations, he is developing a sense of proportion, he is learning to think vitally. The old method in arithmetic left the statement "two times one is two" a cold mathematical fact; the new method makes it a key to living relations. One in the "tables" of the child in mathematics to-day stands for a definite object, and the statement "two times one is two" is an interesting and significant fact. The statement through imaginative thinking, which is vital thinking, may be invested with personal significance and become a personally interesting fact. Try it! Say your "tables of one" up to ten times one is ten, thinking vitally, which means getting behind the statement of the relation to the relation itself, behind the sign to the thing signified. Let your "one" stand each time for something you desire--as a small boy might desire pieces of candy, or a miser "pieces of eight"; now think vitally in this way and say, "Ten times one is ten!" What has happened to the mathematical fact? It has become a living expression!

This might be called interpreting our mathematics. Why not? That is the surest way to master them! It is the surest way to mastery of any subject, of any art, of Life itself. It is the only real way. But we have leaped from the part to the whole, from the study of a detail to an application of the law governing the whole subject. Back we must go to our special point. If we can turn the statement of a cold mathematical fact into the expression of a living vital relation by thinking vitally, so investing the fact with personal significance and making it our own, what can we not do with the more easily appropriated thought which poets and philosophers and play-writers have given us, and with which rests our especial concern as interpreters? Let us see what we can do! But first there is one other point to be considered in this question of vital thinking. We have spoken of one aspect of the process of the mind in thinking,--the concentration upon an idea until it is one's own. But there is the passing of the mind from idea to idea to be noted. This phase the psychologists name "transition." This alternate concentration and transition constitutes the "pulsing of the mind" in reading, which Doctor Curry discusses so vitally in his Lessons in Vocal Expression. Now transition is an inevitable result of concentration and follows it as naturally as expiration follows inspiration. This being true, we need only note, in our study of the process of the mind in reading aloud, the question of transition, letting it follow naturally the fundamental act of concentration which is our chief concern. If the intense concentration is accomplished the clean transition will follow. In choosing material which shall require for adequate interpretation this intense concentration of the mind, we find our source, of course, to be the literature of thought rather than the literature of feeling. The literary form which seems to furnish the best examples for our purpose at this point is the essay where the appeal is, primarily, at least, an intellectual appeal. For my own suggestive analysis and for our preliminary study in vital thinking I have chosen paragraphs from Emerson's essays because Emerson's almost every paragraph is an essay in miniature. The story is told of the gentle seer that once in the midst of a lecture he dropped all the pages of his manuscript over the front of the pulpit. The incident disturbed his auditors greatly until they saw Mr. Emerson gather up the leaves and without any effort at rearrangement in the old order begin to read as though nothing had happened. Every sentence was almost equally pertinent to the main theme, and suffered not from a new juxtaposition. So in printing extracts from this source we feel no sense of incompleteness.

SUGGESTIVE ANALYSIS

Let us read this passage from Emerson's Experience:

To finish the moment, to find the journey's end in every step of the road, to live the greatest number of good hours, is wisdom. It is not the part of men, but of fanatics--or of mathematicians, if you will--to say that, the shortness of life considered, it is not worth caring whether for so short a duration we were sprawling in want or sitting high. Since our office is with moments, let us husband them. Five minutes of to-day are worth as much to me as five minutes in the next millennium. Let us be poised, and wise, and our own, to-day. I settle myself ever the firmer in the creed that we should not postpone and refer and wish, but do broad justice where we are, by whomsoever we deal with, accepting our actual companions and circumstances, however humble or odious, as the mystic officials to whom the universe has delegated its whole pleasure for us.

If you do not think your way through this paragraph clearly, concisely, logically, intensely, when you read it aloud your voice will betray you. In what way? Your tone will lack resonance, your speech will lack precision, your pitch will be monotonous, your touch will be uncertain, your inflections will be indefinite. Your reading will be unconvincing, because it will fail in lucidity and variety. In approaching this passage let us study first the question of proper emphasis. What is emphasis? The dictionaries tell us that, in delivery, it is a special stress of the voice on a given word. But we must use it in a broader sense than this. To emphasize a word is not merely to put a special stress of the voice upon that word. Such an attack might only make the word conspicuous and so defeat the aim of true emphasis. True emphasis is the art of voicing the words in a phrase so that they shall assume a right relation to one another and, so related, best suggest the thought of which they are the symbols. I do not emphasize one word in a phrase and not the others. I simply vary my stress upon each word, in order to gain the proper perspective for the whole sentence. Just so, in a picture, I make one object stand out, and others fall into the background, by drawing or painting them in proper relation to one another. I may use any or all of the "elements of vocal expression" to give that proper relation of values to the words in a single phrase. I may pause, change my pitch, vary my inflection, and alter my tone-color, in order to give a single word its full value. Let us try experiments in emphasis with some isolated sentences before analyzing the longer passage. Here is one of Robert Louis Stevenson's beautifully wrought periods:

"Every man has a sane spot somewhere."

Let us vary, vocally, the relative values of the words in this sentence, and study the effect upon the character of the thought. Let us look upon the statement as a theme for discussion. With a pause before the second word, "man," a lift of the voice on that word, a whimsical turn of the tone, and a significant inflection, we may convert an innocent statement of fact into an incendiary question for debate on the comparative sanity of the sexes. A plea for endless faith and charity becomes a back-handed criticism of women. Now let us read the sentence, giving it its true meaning. "Every man has a sane spot somewhere." Let your voice make of the statement a plea, by dwelling a bit on the first word and again on the last word. Hyphenate the first two words (they really stand for one idea). Compound also the words "sane" and "spot." Lift them as a single word above the rest of the sentence. Now put "somewhere" a little higher still above the level of the rest of the sentence. So, only, have we the true import of this group of words:

some

where.

sane-spot

Everyman has a

Analyze the rest of these sentences from Stevenson in the same way, and experiment with them vocally.

That is never a bad wind that blows where we want to go.

For truth that is suppressed by friends is the readiest weapon of the enemy.

Some strand of our own misdoing is involved in every quarrel.

Drama is the poetry of conduct, romance the poetry of circumstance.

You cannot run away from a weakness; you must sometime fight it out or perish; and if that be so, why not now, and where you stand?

An aim in life is the only fortune worth the finding; and it is not to be found in foreign lands, but in the heart itself.

The world was not made for us; it was made for ten hundred millions of me, all different from each other and from us; there's no royal road, we just have to sclamber and tumble.

Now, once more, and this time with detailed analysis, let us study the passage from Experience. Let us first consider for a moment some of the words which make this passage powerful: finish, journey's-end, good hours, wisdom, fanatics, mathematicians, sprawling-in-want, sitting-high, firmer, poised, postpone, justice, humble, odious, mystic, pleasure. When spoken with a keen sense of its inherent meaning, with full appreciation of its form, and with delight in molding it, how efficient each one of these words becomes! When shall we, as a people, learn reverence for the words which make up our language--reverence that shall make us ashamed to mangle words, offering as our excuse that we are "Westerners" or "Southerners" or from New York or New England or Indiana. The clear-cut thought calls for the clean-cut speech. Let us say these words over and over until they assume full value. And now we pass from words to groups of words. The mind and the tone must move progressively through the first three phrases which make up this first sentence: "To finish the moment, to find the journey's end in every step of the road, to live the greatest number of good hours, is wisdom." The phrases must be held together by an almost imperceptible suspension and upward reach of the voice at the end of each group of words, and yet each phrase must be allowed to be momentarily complete. Read the sentence, making each phrase a conclusion, and then again letting each phrase look forward to the next. Each phrase is really a substantive, looking forward to its predicate through a second substantive which is a little more vital than the first, and again through a third substantive which is a little more vital than either of the other two. Bring this out in reading the sentence. The next sentence depends for its significance upon your contrasting inflections of the three words "men," "fanatics," and "mathematicians"; and again upon your sympathetic inflection of "sprawling-in-want" and "sitting-high." "It is not the part of men, but of fanatics--or of mathematicians, if you will--to say that, the shortness of life considered, it is not worth caring whether for so short a duration we were sprawling in want or sitting high." In your utterance of these words can you make "men" MEN, and "fanatics" fanatics, and consign "mathematicians" to the cold corner of human affairs designed for them? Can you so inflect "sprawling in want" and "sitting high" as to suggest a swamp and a mountain-top, or a frog and an angel? Let your voice leap from the swamp to the mountain-top. Let it climb. Now comes the swift, concise, admonitory sentence: "Since our office is with moments, let us husband them." Pause before you speak the word "husband," and husband it. "Five minutes of to-day are worth as much to me as five minutes in the next millennium." Make "five minutes of to-day" one word, and accent the last syllable, thus: five-minutes-of-to-day. Let the tone retard and take its time on the last seven words. Now poise your tone for the next sentence. "Let us be poised, and wise, and our own, to-day." The paragraph closes with a more complex statement of the theme. Let your voice search out the meaning. Let it settle down into the conclusion, and utter it convincingly. Give a definite touch to the words which I shall put in italics. "I settle myself ever firmer in the creed that we should not *postpone and refer and wish*, but *do broad-justice where we are, by whomsoever we deal with*, accepting our actual companions and circumstances, however humble or odious, as *the mystic officials to whom the universe has dedicated its whole pleasure for us*."

Analyze vocally the following paragraph:

There is a time in every man's education when he arrives at the conviction that envy is ignorance; that imitation is suicide; that he must take himself for better for worse as his portion; that though the wide universe is full of good, no kernel of nourishing corn can come to him but through his toil bestowed on that plot of ground which is given to him to till. The power which resides in him is new in nature, and none but he knows what that is which he can do, nor does he know until he has tried.... What I must do is all that concerns me, not what the people think. This rule, equally arduous in actual and in intellectual life, may serve for the whole distinction between greatness and meanness. It is the harder because you will always find those who think they know what is your duty better than you know it. It is easy in the world to live after the world's opinion; it is easy in solitude to live after our own; but the great man is he who in the midst of the crowd keeps with perfect sweetness the independence of solitude.--Self-Reliance.

SELECTIONS FOR INTERPRETATION

By choosing as further material for vocal interpretation selections which shall also be good examples for examination as to their literary construction, we shall serve the double purpose of adapting our studies in vocal interpretation to the uses of English composition.

The following selections are to be: first, read aloud (in class); second, examined as to their literary construction (in class); third, analyzed and reported upon as specimens of exposition and argumentation (in the study).

Exposition is an explanation, a setting forth, or an expounding. It is an attempt to render something plain, an effort to convey to the reader a train of thought which represents the conclusions of the writer upon a subject. The writer, it is at once evident, must be acquainted with the subject with which he deals. He is presuming to teach, and must be in a position which justifies him in so doing. He is prepared to write an exposition only when he is able, in regard to the topic in hand, to take frankly and unreservedly the attitude of a teacher.

A teacher must have many good gifts and graces; and whoever else may fail to be well acquainted with a given lesson, he must have mastered it thoroughly. To teach he must first know. Whoever has taught understands how completely different is the attitude of the teacher from that of the pupil. While the pupil is hardly expected to be able to do more than reasonably well to understand the subject in hand, the teacher must be able to explain, to justify, to make clear relations, and to impart the whole matter. The pupil is excused with a sort of hearsay knowledge, but the teacher must have a vital experience of what he teaches. Especially must he be able to comprehend and to represent a subject as a whole. He is responsible for the student's being able in turn to co-ordinate facts and theories so as to produce unity; and it is therefore essential that he himself have power to hold and to make clear a continuous train of thought.

The teacher, moreover, must have over his mind discipline so firm that he is not dependent upon moods. He must cover the wide difference between the train of thought which springs spontaneously in the mind and that which is laboriously worked out as a logical sequence of ideas relating to a subject forced upon the attention. The pupil may, to a certain extent, indulge the vagaries of his inclination, but the teacher must respond to the need of the moment. He must have trained his mind to give an intelligent judgment upon any matter presented to it. He is not equipped for instructing--nor is any individual ready for life--until he can command the resources of his inner self to the utmost. The trained person is one who can take a subject which may not at the outset especially appeal to him, which is full of complications, which is not in itself, perhaps, attractive, and can insist with himself that his mind shall master it thoroughly. He is able so to expend his whole mental strength, if need be, upon any necessary topic that the subject shall be examined, acquired, assimilated, and then shall be so organized, so illumined, and so presented that others shall be instructed. The mind of the teacher, in a word, is so disciplined that it will work when it is ordered.

The ideal state of mind for him who wishes to communicate knowledge is that of being absolute master of all its resources. Many who possess no inconsiderable powers of thought are practically unable to command the best powers of their intelligence. They depend upon the whim of the moment, upon some outward pressure or inward impulse, to arouse their intellect. They fail to reflect that while any ordinary intellect naturally forms some opinion upon any subject which interests it, only the trained mind is able to judge clearly and lucidly of an indifferent or uninteresting matter. In this mastery of thought lies the difference between the sterile and the productive mind. Only one brain in a thousand has not the disposition to shirk work if it is allowed, and every student has moments when his intelligence seems almost to act like a spoiled child that hates to get up when called on a cold morning. To establish the power of the will over the intellect is the object of education, and the ability to exercise this power is what is meant by the proper use of the word "cultivation."

The mental process of the cultivated thinker when considering any subject is likely to be: first, to become sure of his terms; then, clearly to set before his mind the facts and conditions; and, lastly, to make the possible and resulting deductions and conclusions. This gives a hint, and indeed practically affords a rule for the writer of exposition.

An exposition, broadly speaking, may be said to consist of three steps which nearly correspond to the three steps of mental activity just set down: the Definition, the Statement, and the Inference.

Definition is making clear to self or to the reader what is under discussion.

Statement is the setting forth of whatever is to be said of the facts, conditions, relations, and so on, which it is the object of the exposition to make clear.

Inference is the conclusion or conclusions drawn.

These three parts will seldom be found as formal divisions in any ordinary exposition, but in some sort they are always present; and the writer must at least have them clear in his mind if he hopes to render his work well ordered, comprehensive, and symmetrical. Together they are woven as the strands which give a firmness of texture to the whole.

To illustrate the bearing of this analysis on the composition of an exposition, we may imagine that a student has been required to write a theme on "The Influence of College Life." He has first to concern himself with definition. He must decide what he means by college life as a molding influence; whether its intellectual, its social, its moral aspects, or all these. He must consider, too, whether he is to deal with the effect upon specific characters or upon types; whether upon boys during the time they are in college or as a training for after life; whether at a special institution or as the result of any college. If he limits himself to one phase of influence, he must in the same way decide fully in what sense he intends to treat that phase. If he is to consider the social effect of college life, for instance, he has to define for himself the sense in which he will use the word "social." Is it to mean simply formal society, adaptation to the more conventional and exclusive forms of human intercourse, or to imply all that renders a man more self-poised, more flexible, and more adaptable in any relations with his fellows? If, on the other hand, it is the intellectual influence of college life which is to be studied, the first step is to decide what is to be considered for this purpose the range of the term "intellectual"; whether it is to be taken to mean the mere acquirement of information; whether it has relation to acquirement or to modification of mental conditions; whether it means change in the mind in the way of development or of modification; whether it shall be applied to an alteration in the student's attitude toward knowledge or toward life in general. All this is in the line of definition, and it is naturally connected with the statement of whatever facts bear upon the topic under discussion.

Statement has largely to do with fact. Theory belongs rather to whatever inference is part of an exposition. In the statement will come the observations of the writer; whatever he knows of general conditions at college, or such individual examples as bear upon the question in hand. From these he will inevitably draw some conclusions, and the value of the exposition will depend upon the reasonableness and convincingness of these inferences, as these will, in turn, depend upon the clearness of the writer's original knowledge in regard to his intentions and the logic of his statements.

Composition, it should be remembered, is the art of communicating to others what is in the mind of the writer. To write without having the subject abundantly in mind is to invite the reader to a Barmecide feast of empty dishes. The necessity of insisting upon such particulars as those just given of the process of making an exposition arises from the stubborn idea of the untrained student that writing is something done with paper and ink. It is, on the contrary, something which is done with brains; it is less putting things on paper than it is thinking things out in the mind.

Before leaving the illustration of a theme on the influence of college life we may glance a moment more at the difficulty, even with so simple a subject, of attaining perfect clarity of thinking. One of the first things which must be determined is the essential difference of life in a college from ordinary existence. If the subject be given out to a class of students half the themes handed in will begin with a remark upon the great change which comes to a boy who finds himself for the first time freed from the restraints of home. The moment this idea is presented to the mind it is to be looked at, not as something with which to fill so much paper, but as a stepping-stone toward ideas beyond. It is necessary, for instance, to determine the distinctions between freedom at college and freedom elsewhere; to decide wherein lie the differences in the conditions which surround a boy in a university and one who escapes from the restrictions of home by going away to live in a city or in a country village, on shipboard or in the army. To be of value, every thought in an exposition must have been tested by a comparison with allied ideas as wide and as exhaustive as the thinker is equal to making.

To learn to think is, after all, the prime essential in exposition-writing, and the beginning of thought is the realization of what is already known. The student who patiently examines his views on the subject of which he is to write, who determines to discover exactly how much he knows and what is the relative importance of each of his opinions, is likely soon to come to find that he is considering the theme chosen not only deeply, but with tangible results. The value of any exposition, to sum the matter up in a word, rests primarily and chiefly on the thoroughness of the thought which produces it.-- ARLO BATES.[3]

[3] This selection from Prof. Arlo Bates's Talks on Writing English is printed by permission of the author and his publishers, Houghton Mifflin Company.

The Idylls of the King has been called a quasi-epic. Departing from the conventional epic form by its lack of a closely continuous narrative, it has yet that lofty manner and underlying unity of design which leads us to class it with the epics, at least, in the essentials. It consists of a series of chivalric legends, taken chiefly from the Morte d'Arthur of Sir Thomas Malory, grouped so as to exhibit the establishment, the greatness, and the downfall of an ideal kingdom of righteousness among men. "The Coming of Arthur," the ideal ruler, shows us the setting up of this kingdom. Before this was disorder, great tracts of wilderness,

Wherein the beast was ever more and more, But man was less and less.

Arthur slays the beast and fells the forest, and the old order changes to give place to new. Then the song of Arthur's knights rises, a majestic chorus of triumph:

Clang battle-axe and clash brand. Let the king reign.

In "Gareth and Lynette" the newly established kingdom is seen doing its work among men. Arthur, enthroned in his great hall, dispenses impartial justice. The knights

Ride abroad redressing human wrongs.

The allegory shows us, in Gareth's contests with the knights "that have no law nor King," the contest of the soul with the temptations that at different periods of life successively attack it:

The war of Time against the soul of man.

Then follow the "Idylls," which trace the entrance and growth of an element of sin and discord, which, spreading, pulls down into ruin that "fellowship of noble knights," "which are an image of the mighty world." The purity of the ideal kingdom is fouled, almost at its source, by the guilty love of Lancelot and the Queen. Among some the contagion spreads; while others, in an extremity of protest, start in quest of the Holy Grail, leaving the duty at hand for mystical visions. Man cannot bring down heaven to earth; he cannot sanctify the mass of men by his own rapturous anticipations; he cannot safely neglect the preliminary stages of progress appointed for the race; he "may not wander from the allotted field before his work be done."

So by impurity and by impatience the rift in the kingdom widens, and in "The Last Tournament," in the stillness before the impending doom, we hear the shrill voice of Dagonet railing at the King, who thinks himself as God, that he can make

Honey from hornet-combs And men from beasts.

In "Guinevere," unequaled elsewhere in the "Idylls" in pure poetry, the blow falls; at length, in the concluding poem, Arthur passes to the isle of Avilion, and once more

The old order changeth, yielding place to new.

Tennyson himself tells us that in this, his longest poem, he has meant to shadow "sense at war with soul," the struggle in the individual and in the race, between that body which links us with the brute and the soul which makes us part of a spiritual order. But the mastery of the higher over the lower is only obtained through many seeming failures. Wounded and defeated, the King exclaims:

For I, being simple, thought to work His will, And have but stricken with the sword in vain; And all whereon I lean'd, in wife and friend, Is traitor to my peace, and all my realm Reels back into the beast, and is no more.

But he also half perceives the truth which it is the poet's purpose to suggest to us. It is short-sighted to expect the immediate sanctification of the race; if we are disheartened, striving to "work His will," it is because "we see not the close." It is impossible that Arthur's work should end in failure--departing, he declares, "I pass, but shall not die," and when his grievous wound is healed, he will return. The Idylls of the King is thus the epic of evolution in application to the progress of human society. In it the teachings of "In Memoriam" assume a narrative form.

Move upward, working out the beast,

may be taken as a brief statement of its theme: and we read in it the belief in the tendency upward and an assurance of ultimate triumph:

Oh, yet we trust that somehow good Will be the final goal of ill, To pangs of nature, sins of will, Defects of doubt, and taints of blood;

That nothing walks with aimless feet, That not one life shall be destroyed, Or cast as rubbish to the void When God hath made the pile complete.

--PANCOAST.[4]

As an interlude study which shall look back to the step we have just taken, and forward to the one we are about to take, let us test our growth in vitality in thinking and our need of intelligence in feeling, by voicing the following selections from didactic poetry. This form affords the best exercise in both activities because it makes a double appeal, and so a double demand upon the interpreter--an appeal through form to emotion, through aim to intelligence, and through message and atmosphere to both. I have chosen examples of this form in which the beauty and fascination of meter, rhythm, and rhyme, and the didactic nature of the thought do not seem to overbalance each other. If either should predominate you must, by your interpretation, strike the balance. In reading Robert Browning's Rabbi Ben Ezra (from which I shall quote but a few verses) you must carry to your auditor the full import of the philosophy, but in doing so you must not lose the beauty of the verse in which the poet has set it.

RABBI BEN EZRA

Grow old along with me! The best is yet to be, The last of life, for which the first was made: Our times are in His hand Who saith, "A whole I planned, Youth shows but half; trust God: see all, nor be afraid!"

Not that, amassing flowers, Youth sighed, "Which rose make ours, Which lily leave and then as best recall?" Not that, admiring stars, It yearned, "Nor Jove, nor Mars; Mine be some figured flame which blends, transcends them all!"

Not for such hopes and fears Annulling youth's brief years, Do I remonstrate: folly wide the mark! Rather I prize the doubt Low kinds exist without, Finished and finite clods, untroubled by a spark.

* * * * *

Then, welcome each rebuff That turns earth's smoothness rough, Each sting that bids nor sit nor stand but go! Be our joys three-parts pain! Strive and hold cheap the strain, Learn, nor account the pang; dare, never grudge the throe!

For thence--a paradox Which comforts while it mocks-- Shall life succeed in that it seems to fail: What I aspired to be, And was not, comforts me: A brute I might have been, but would not sink i' the scale.

* * * * *

Now, who shall arbitrate? Ten men love what I hate, Shun what I follow, slight what I receive; Ten, who in ears and eyes Match me: we all surmise, They, this thing, and I, that: whom shall my soul believe?

Not on the vulgar mass Called "work," must sentence pass, Things done, that took the eye and had the price; O'er which, from level stand, The low world laid its hand, Found straightway to its mind, could value in a trice:

But all, the world's coarse thumb And finger failed to plumb, So passed in making up the main account: All instincts immature, All purposes unsure, That weighed not as his work, yet swelled the man's amount:

Thoughts hardly to be packed Into a narrow act, Fancies that broke through language and escaped; All I could never be, All, men ignored in me, This, I was worth to God, whose wheel the pitcher shaped.

* * * * *

--BROWNING.

FORBEARANCE

Hast thou named all the birds without a gun? Loved the wood-rose, and left it on its stalk? At rich men's tables eaten bread and pulse? Unarmed, faced danger with a heart of trust? And loved so well a high behavior, In man or maid, that thou from speech refrained, Nobility more nobly to repay? O, be my friend, and teach me to be thine!

EACH AND ALL

Little thinks, in the field, yon red-cloaked clown Of thee from the hill-top looking down; The heifer that lows in the upland farm, Far-heard, lows not thine ear to charm; The sexton, tolling his bell at noon, Deems not that great Napoleon Stops his horse and lists with delight, Whilst his files sweep round yon Alpine height; Nor knowest thou what argument Thy life to thy neighbor's creed has lent. All are needed by each one; Nothing is fair or good alone. I thought the sparrow's note from heaven, Singing at dawn on the alder bough; I brought him home, in his nest, at even; He sings the song, but it cheers not now, For I did not bring home the river and sky;-- He sang to my ear,--they sang to my eye. The delicate shells lay on the shore; The bubbles of the latest wave Fresh pearls to their enamel gave, And the bellowing of the savage sea Greeted their safe escape to me. I wiped away the weeds and foam, I fetched my sea-born treasures home; But the poor, unsightly, noisome things Had left their beauty on the shore With the sun and the sand and the wild uproar. The lover watched his graceful maid, As 'mid the virgin train she strayed, Nor knew her beauty's best attire Was woven still by the snow-white choir. At last she came to his hermitage, Like the bird from the woodlands to the cage;-- The gay enchantment was undone, A gentle wife, but fairy none. Then I said, "I covet truth; Beauty is unripe childhood's cheat; I leave it behind with the games of youth":-- As I spoke, beneath my feet The ground-pine curled its pretty wreath, Running over the club-moss burrs; I inhaled the violet's breath; Around me stood the oaks and firs; Pine-cones and acorns lay on the ground; Over me soared the eternal sky, Full of light and of deity; Again I saw, again I heard, The rolling river, the morning bird;-- Beauty through my senses stole; I yielded myself to the perfect whole.

--EMERSON.

As a final step in this study which has for its aim an increase in your power to think vitally you are to choose from the "great heap of your knowledge" a subject about which you have sufficient understanding and enthusiasm to justify your discussion of it, and with this as a topic you are "to unmuzzle your wisdom" in the form of exposition or argumentation.

SECOND STUDY

TO ESTABLISH INTELLIGENCE IN FEELING

Art is in bondage in this country: its internal polity to the temperamental ideal; its external polity to the commercial ideal. Business and social life are in the same bondage. In music, in drama, in letters, in society, and in trade we permit personality to exploit itself for commercial purposes. The result is either chaotic or calculated expression on every side. When temperament seeks restraint in technique, and policy, whether business or social, seeks freedom in service, then shall we have that balanced expression in art, in society, and in trade which should proceed from the American personality and distinguish American life.

It may seem a far cry from a comment upon American life to the subject of this second study--intelligence in feeling. Carry the idea of balanced expression from the introduction to the body of this exposition and the transition is not difficult to make.

"Wonderful technique, but no heart in her singing!" "Tremendous temperament, but no technique!" "She moves me profoundly, but oh, what a method!" "Her instrument is flawless, but she leaves me absolutely unmoved." Have you ever heard such comment, or made such comment, or been the subject of like comment? Diagnosis of the case, whether it be yours or another's, should be the same--lack of poise in expression, producing the undesirable effect upon the auditor of no emotion at all, or of unintelligent emotion. To determine just what we mean by intelligent emotion is our first problem for this study.

An experience I had in visiting a class in interpretation in a well-known school of oratory some years ago will illustrate the point. The selection for interpretation was the prelude to the first part of The Vision of Sir Launfal.

"And what is so rare as a day in June? Then, if ever, come perfect days; Then Heaven tries earth if it be in tune, And over it softly her warm ear lays; ..."

The work was well under way when I entered the class-room. My entrance did not disturb the expression on the face of the student who was "up before" the class. A Malvolio smile was never more deliciously indelible. I thought at first my request to see some work in interpretation had been mistaken and I had been ushered into a class in facial gymnastics. Then I concluded that Mr. Lowell's poem was being employed as text for an exercise in smiling. Finally the awful truth came upon me that this teacher of interpretation was seriously attempting to secure from her pupils an expression which should suggest the spirit of the June day by asking them to assume the outward sign of joy known as smiling. The result was a ghastly series of facial contortions, which left at least one auditor's day as bleak as the bleakest December. No intelligent feeling can be induced in interpreter or auditor by assuming the outward sign of an inward emotion. Some of you are recalling Mr. James's talk to students, on the reflex theory of emotion, and are being confused at this point. Let us stop and straighten out the confusion. Mr. James says:

"Action seems to follow feeling, but really action and feeling go together; and by regulating the action, which is under the more direct control of the will, we can indirectly regulate the feeling, which is not.

"Thus the sovereign voluntary path to cheerfulness, if our spontaneous cheerfulness be lost, is to sit up cheerfully, to look round cheerfully, and to act and speak as if cheerfulness were already there. If such conduct does not make you soon feel cheerful, nothing else on that occasion can. So to feel brave, act as if we were brave, use all our will to that end, and a courage-fit will very likely replace the fit of fear."

The application of this principle to the reading of these lines would seem to justify the method the teacher was pursuing. A smile is acceptedly the indication of happy emotion, the outward symbol of inward rejoicing or joy. The June day is full of joyful emotion,--the joy of awakening life. Applying Mr. James's theory, a legitimate way to induce the inward emotion would seem to be to assume the outward sign. But wait a moment. Let us look to our premises. Mr. Lanier, who sings of Nature with joyful understanding, cries in Sunrise:

"Tell me, sweet burly-bark'd, man-bodied Tree That mine arms in the dark are embracing, dost know From what fount are these tears at thy feet which flow? They rise not from reason, but deeper inconsequent deeps. Reason's not one that weeps. What logic of greeting lies Betwixt dear over-beautiful trees and the rain of the eyes?"

Here is a great master of verbal expression whose inward joy finds its outward symbol not in a smile but in a tear. So you and I may respond to Mr. Lowell's "high tide of the year" with smiles or with tears, with bowed head and closed eyes, or with eyes wide and head raised to meet the returning flood of life.

The effect upon me of the beauty of this day as Mr. Lowell has painted it, my personal emotional response is interesting psychology, but is not my concern as an interpreter. My own emotion and its personal response belong to my preparatory interpretative efforts in the study; but when the interpretation is ready for the audience-room, the emotion must be assimilated into the interpretative act and appear only as part of the illumination of the bit of life I am presenting.

The object of all great art, whether creative or interpretative, is not to exploit the personality of the artist, but to disclose at some point the personality of the very God himself, which is life. The revelation not of personal emotion but of universal life is the legitimate aim of all artistic effort.

Emotional response will accompany every vital mental conception. Abandonment to that response is a legitimate and necessary part of full comprehension. But such abandonment, as I have said, belongs to our preparation for expression. Such abandonment must not be taken out of the study on to the stage. No temperamental expression along any line is fit for the public until it is controlled by technique, the technique which has been worked out by the masters of every art, not excluding the art of living.

It is not the effect of June upon you I want from your interpretation, it is the spirit of June itself. You must let me have my own emotion. Your emotional response was the result of your mental concept; mine, to be intelligent, must find the same impulse. If you impose your own emotion upon me mine will be merely an unintelligent reflection of yours. Taking as our ideal of the interpreter, the absolutely pure medium, bars out every manifestation which calls attention to the interpreter, and so interferes with the direct message.

"The natural form of expression which literature takes when it passes beyond the normal powers of prose, is lyric poetry. When your feelings rise beyond a certain degree of stress you need the stronger beat and vibration of verse; to express the highest joy or the deepest grief poetry is your natural instrument." Again corroborated in our choice of direction in study by Mr. Gardiner, let us turn for "material" in the establishment of intelligence in emotion, to the most intensive type of the literature of feeling,--lyric poetry.

"Every now and then a man will come who will reduce to words--as Mr. Ruskin has done--some impression of vivid pleasure which has never been reduced to words before. It is only the great master who makes these advances; by studying his works you may perhaps come somewhere near the mark that he has set." This further word from the same paragraph should influence us to pause with Mr. Ruskin's poetry in prose form for a brief study on our way to the lyrics of Wordsworth and Shelley and Keats, a song from Shakespeare, and some few from the rare, more modern lyricists. I shall trust you to this by-path under the guidance of The Forms of Prose Literature, where you will find passages from such masters of prose as Mr. Ruskin and Mr. Stevenson--passages of surpassing lyric beauty which shall furnish models for your correlated study in Description.

SUGGESTIVE ANALYSIS

I have chosen for suggestive analysis of the lyric, Shelley's ode To a Skylark. I shall analyze in detail only the first five stanzas:

Hail to thee, blithe Spirit! Bird thou never wert, That from heaven, or near it Pourest thy full heart In profuse strains of unpremeditated art.

Higher still and higher From the earth thou springest, Like a cloud of fire The blue deep thou wingest, And singing still dost soar, and soaring ever singest.

In the golden lightning Of the sunken sun O'er which clouds are brightening, Thou dost float and run, Like an unbodied joy whose race is just begun.

The pale purple even Melts around thy flight; Like a star of heaven In the broad daylight Thou art unseen, but yet I hear thy shrill delight.

Keen as are the arrows Of that silver sphere Whose intense lamp narrows In the white dawn clear, Until we hardly see, we feel that it is there.

How shall we create an atmosphere for the reading of these verses! How can we catch the spirit of the creator of them! Shall we ever feel ready to voice that first line? Do you know Jules Breton's picture The Lark? Do you love it? Go, then, and stand before it, actually or in imagination. Let something of the spirit which informs that lovely child, lifting her eyes, her head in an attitude of listening rapture, steal over you. I know her power. I have tested it. In reading the "Skylark" with a class of boys and girls from twelve to fourteen years old, I tried the experiment. I happened to have with me a beautiful copy of Breton's picture. I took it to the class-room. I wrote on the blackboard verses of the poem and hung the picture over them. The picture taught them to read the poem. The eyes of the girl became their teacher. I tried the experiment, with a private pupil in my studio, with a somewhat different result. I had told her to bring a copy of Shelley's poems to her next lesson. "Do you know the ode To a Skylark?" I asked. "Yes," she said. A copy of Breton's picture hung on the wall. "Before you open your book look at the picture," I said. She obeyed. Her expression, always radiant, deepened its radiance. "Do you know what the girl is doing?" I asked. "Oh yes, she is listening to the skylark." "How do you know?" "I have heard the skylark sing." "I never have," I said. "Read the poem to me." Now when I read the "Skylark," I see the girl in Jules Breton's picture, but I hear the voice of my English pupil.

But if our apperceptive background fails to furnish a memory of the identical sight and sound for our inspiring, it at least holds bird notes and bird flights of great beauty, and we must call upon these for the impulse to voice Shelley's apostrophe:

Hail to thee, blithe Spirit! Bird thou never wert, That from heaven, or near it Pourest thy full heart In profuse strains of unpremeditated art.

An early autumn number of the Atlantic Monthly for 1907 published a poem by Mr. Ridgley Torrence, entitled The Lesser Children, or A Threnody at the Hunting Season. The poem is worthy, in sentiment and structure, to be set beside Shelley's ode. Let us compare with the picture which the eighteenth-century poet has given us this one from our modern song-writer:

Who has not seen in the high gulf of light What, lower, was a bird, but now Is moored and altered quite Into an island of unshaded joy? To whom the mate below upon the bough Shouts once and brings him from his high employ. Yet speeding he forgot not of the cloud Where he from glory sprang and burned aloud, But took a little of the day, A little of the colored sky, And of the joy that would not stay He wove a song that cannot die.

Now let us study closely the first verse of the older poem. Spirit and voice must soar in the first line, "Hail to thee, blithe Spirit!" The two words "hail" and "blithe" are swift-winged words. Let them fly. Give them their wings. Let them do all they are intended to do. The rhythm of the whole poem is aspiring. Reverence the rhythm, but keep the thought floating clear above it in the second line, "Bird thou never wert." With the next two lines the tone must gather head to be poured forth in the last line, "In profuse strains of unpremeditated art." Let us make another comparative study. Set on the other side of this picture Lowell's description of the "little bird" in his prologue to Sir Launfal's vision:

The little bird sits at his door in the sun, Atilt like a blossom among the leaves, And lets his illumined being o'errun With the deluge of summer it receives.

The second verse of the "Skylark" demands a still higher flight of imagination and tone. Let us try it.

Higher still and higher From the earth thou springest, Like a cloud of fire The blue deep thou wingest, And singing still dost soar, and soaring ever singest.

Again all the words rise and float. Sing them over: higher, higher, springest, fire, wingest, singing, soar, soaring, singest. The reader must feel himself poised for flight in every word of the first three verses. Why does the poet say cloud of fire? What is the color of the skylark? And now the tone, which has been of a radiant hue through these three verses, must soften a little in the first three lines of the next verse--

The pale purple even Melts around thy flight;--

glow gold again in the last three lines--

Like a star of heaven In the broad daylight Thou art unseen, and yet I hear thy shrill delight--

and become the white of an incandescent light in the next verse--

Keen as are the arrows Of that silver sphere Whose intense lamp narrows In the white dawn clear, Until we hardly see, we feel that it is there.

Do you not see that the secret of its beauty lies, for vocal interpretation, in the color of tone and in the inflection of the words? Say "unseen," dwelling on the second syllable; "shrill delight," directing shrill over the head of delight; "keen," making it cleave the air like an arrow; "silver sphere," suggesting a moonlit path across water; "intense" and "narrows," letting the tone recede into the "white dawn"; "see," with a vanishing stress; and "feel," with a deepening note carried to the end. So we might go on through the twenty-one stanzas which make up the poem.

Please analyze undirected the next two verses.

All the earth and air With thy voice is loud, As, when night is bare, From one lonely cloud The moon rains out her beams, and heaven is overflow'd.

What thou art we know not; What is most like thee? From rainbow clouds there flow not Drops so bright to see As from thy presence showers a rain of melody.

In reading the first lines of the next four verses we must avoid monotony.

Like a poet hidden In the light of thought, Singing hymns unbidden, Till the world is wrought To sympathy with hopes and fears it heeded not:

Like a high-born maiden In a palace tower, Soothing her love-laden Soul in secret hour With music sweet as love, which overflows her bower:

Like a glowworm golden In a dell of dew, Scattering unbeholden Its aerial hue Among the flowers and grass, which screen it from the view:

Like a rose embower'd In its own green leaves, By warm winds deflower'd, Till the scent it gives Makes faint with too much sweet these heavy-winged thieves.

Vary, if only for variety, the pitch on which you begin each of these first lines. Let the first three words of the eighth verse, "like a poet," ascend in pitch. Keep the voice level in the first line of the ninth verse, "like a high-born maiden." Let the pitch fall in the first words of the tenth stanza, "like a glowworm golden." And again keep the tone level on the first line of the next stanza, "like a rose embower'd." I leave to you the analysis of the rest of the poem:

Sound of vernal showers On the twinkling grass, Rain-awaken'd flowers, All that ever was Joyous, and clear, and fresh, thy music doth surpass.

Teach us, sprite or bird, What sweet thoughts are thine: I have never heard Praise of love or wine That panted forth a flood of rapture so divine.

Chorus hymeneal Or triumphal chaunt Match'd with thine, would be all But an empty vaunt-- A thing wherein we feel there is some hidden want.

What objects are the fountains Of thy happy strain? What field, or waves, or mountains? What shapes of sky or plain? What love of thine own kind? what ignorance of pain?

With thy clear, keen joyance Languor cannot be: Shadow of annoyance Never came near thee: Thou lovest; but ne'er knew love's sad satiety.

Waking or asleep Thou of death must deem Things more true and deep Than we mortals dream, Or how could thy notes flow in such a crystal stream?

We look before and after, And pine for what is not: Our sincerest laughter With some pain is fraught; Our sweetest songs are those that tell of saddest thought.

Yet if we could scorn Hate and pride and fear; If we were things born Not to shed a tear, I know not how thy joy we ever should come near.

Better than all measures Of delightful sound, Better than all treasures That in books are found, Thy skill to poet were, thou scorner of the ground!

Teach me half the gladness That thy brain must know, Such harmonious madness From my lips would flow, The world should listen then, as I am listening now!

--SHELLEY.

SELECTIONS FOR INTERPRETATION

The following selections from lyric poetry are designed to give the voice exercise in the expression of varied emotions.

I

THE DAFFODILS

I wander'd lonely as a cloud That floats on high o'er vales and hills, When all at once I saw a crowd, A host of golden daffodils, Beside the lake, beneath the trees, Fluttering and dancing in the breeze.

Continuous as the stars that shine And twinkle on the milky way, They stretch'd in never-ending line Along the margin of a bay: Ten thousand saw I at a glance Tossing their heads in sprightly dance.

The waves beside them danced, but they Out-did the sparkling waves in glee:-- A Poet could not but be gay In such a jocund company! I gazed--and gazed-- but little thought What wealth the show to me had brought;

For oft, when on my couch I lie In vacant or in pensive mood, They flash upon that inward eye Which is the bliss of solitude; And then my heart with pleasure fills, And dances with the daffodils.

--WORDSWORTH.

II

BY THE SEA

It is a beauteous evening, calm and free; The holy time is quiet as a Nun Breathless with adoration; the broad sun Is sinking down in its tranquillity;

The gentleness of heaven is on the Sea: Listen! the mighty Being is awake, And doth with his eternal motion make A sound like thunder--everlastingly.

Dear child! dear girl! that walkest with me here, If thou appear untouch'd by solemn thought Thy nature is not therefore less divine: Thou liest in Abraham's bosom all the year, And worship'st at the Temple's inner shrine, God being with thee when we know it not.

--WORDSWORTH.

III

TO THE CUCKOO

O blithe new-comer! I have heard, I hear thee and rejoice: O Cuckoo! shall I call thee Bird, Or but a wandering Voice?

While I am lying on the grass Thy twofold shout I hear; From hill to hill it seems to pass, At once far off and near.

Though babbling only to the vale Of sunshine and of flowers, Thou bringest unto me a tale Of visionary hours.

Thrice welcome, darling of the Spring! Even yet thou art to me No bird, but an invisible thing, A voice, a mystery;

The same whom in my school-boy days I listen'd to; that Cry Which made me look a thousand ways In bush, and tree, and sky.

To seek thee did I often rove Through woods and on the green; And thou wert still a hope, a love, Still long'd for, never seen!

And I can listen to thee yet, Can lie upon the plain And listen, till I do beget That golden time again.

O blessed Bird! the earth we pace Again appears to be An unsubstantial, faery place, That is fit home for Thee!

IV

ODE TO THE WEST WIND

O wild West Wind, thou breath of Autumn's being, Thou, from whose unseen presence the leaves dead Are driven, like ghosts from an enchanter fleeing, Yellow, and black, and pale, and hectic red, Pestilence-stricken multitudes! O thou Who chariotest to their dark wintry bed The wing 閣 seeds, where they lie cold and low, Each like a corpse within its grave, until Thine azure sister of the Spring shall blow Her clarion o'er the dreaming earth, and fill (Driving sweet buds like flocks to feed in air) With living hues and odours plain and hill: Wild Spirit, which art moving everywhere; Destroyer and Preserver; Hear, oh hear!

Thou on whose stream, 'mid the steep sky's commotion, Loose clouds like earth's decaying leaves are shed, Shook from the tangled boughs of heaven and ocean, Angels of rain and lightning! there are spread On the blue surface of thine airy surge, Like the bright hair uplifted from the head Of some fierce Maenad, ev'n from the dim verge Of the horizon to the zenith's height-- The locks of the approaching storm. Thou dirge Of the dying year, to which this closing night Will be the dome of a vast sepulchre, Vaulted with all thy congregated might Of vapours, from whose solid atmosphere Black rain, and fire, and hail, will burst: Oh hear!

Thou who didst waken from his summer-dreams The blue Mediterranean, where he lay, Lull'd by the coil of his crystalline streams, Beside a pumice isle in Baiae's bay, And saw in sleep old palaces and towers Quivering within the wave's intenser day, All overgrown with azure moss, and flowers So sweet, the sense faints picturing them! Thou For whose path the Atlantic's level powers Cleave themselves into chasms, while far below The sea-blooms and the oozy woods which wear The sapless foliage of the ocean, know Thy voice, and suddenly grow gray with fear And tremble and despoil themselves: Oh hear!

If I were a dead leaf thou mightest bear; If I were a swift cloud to fly with thee; A wave to pant beneath thy power, and share The impulse of thy strength, only less free Than Thou, O uncontrollable! If even I were as in my boyhood, and could be The comrade of thy wanderings over heaven, As then, when to outstrip thy skiey speed Scarce seem'd a vision,--I would ne'er have striven As thus with thee in prayer in my sore need. Oh! lift me as a wave, a leaf, a cloud! I fall upon the thorns of life! I bleed! A heavy weight of hours has chain'd and bow'd One too like thee--tameless, and swift, and proud.

Make me thy lyre, ev'n as the forest is: What if my leaves are falling like its own! The tumult of thy mighty harmonies Will take from both a deep autumnal tone, Sweet though in sadness. Be thou, Spirit fierce, My spirit! be thou me, impetuous one! Drive my dead thoughts over the universe, Like wither'd leaves, to quicken a new birth; And, by the incantation of this verse, Scatter, as from an unextinguish'd hearth Ashes and sparks, my words among mankind! Be through my lips to unawaken'd earth The trumpet of a prophecy! O Wind, If Winter comes, can Spring be far behind?

--SHELLEY.

V

TO THE NIGHT

Swiftly walk over the western wave, Spirit of night! Out of the misty eastern cave Where, all the long and lone daylight, Thou wovest dreams of joy and fear Which make thee terrible and dear,-- Swift be thy flight!

Wrap thy form in a mantle gray Star-inwrought; Blind with thine hair the eyes of Day, Kiss her until she be wearied out: Then wander o'er sea and city and land, Touching all with thine opiate wand-- Come, long-sought!

When I arose and saw the dawn, I sigh'd for thee: When light rode high, and the dew was gone, And noon lay heavy on flower and tree, And the weary Day turn'd to his rest Lingering like an unloved guest, I sigh'd for thee.

Thy brother Death came, and cried Wouldst thou me? Thy sweet child Sleep, the filmy-eyed, Murmur'd like a noon-tide bee Shall I nestle near thy side? Wouldst thou me?--And I replied No, not thee!

Death will come when thou art dead, Soon, too soon-- Sleep will come when thou art fled; Of neither would I ask the boon I ask of thee, beloved Night-- Swift be thine approaching flight, Come soon, soon!

--SHELLEY.

VI

ODE TO A GRECIAN URN

Thou still unravish'd bride of quietness, Thou foster-child of silence and slow time, Sylvan historian, who canst thus express A flowery tale more sweetly than our rhyme: What leaf-fringed legend haunts about thy shape Of deities or mortals, or of both, In Temp?or the dales of Arcady? What men or gods are these? What maidens loth? What mad pursuit? What struggle to escape? What pipes and timbrels? What wild ecstasy?

Heard melodies are sweet, but those unheard Are sweeter; therefore, ye soft pipes, play on; Not to the sensual ear, but, more endear'd, Pipe to the spirit ditties of no tone: Fair youth, beneath the trees, thou canst not leave Thy song, nor ever can those trees be bare; Bold Lover, never, never canst thou kiss, Though winning near the goal--yet, do not grieve; She cannot fade, though thou hast not thy bliss, For ever wilt thou love, and she be fair!

Ah happy, happy boughs! that cannot shed Your leaves, nor ever bid the Spring adieu; And, happy melodist, unweari 閣, For ever piping songs for ever new; More happy love! more happy, happy love! For ever warm and still to be enjoy'd, For ever panting, and for ever young; All breathing human passion far above, That leaves a heart high-sorrowful and cloy'd, A burning forehead, and a parching tongue.

Who are these coming to the sacrifice? To what green altar, O mysterious priest, Lead'st thou that heifer lowing at the skies, And all her silken flanks with garlands drest? What little town by river or sea shore, Or mountain-built with peaceful citadel, Is emptied of this folk, this pious morn? And, little town, thy streets for evermore Will silent be; and not a soul to tell Why thou art desolate, can e'er return.

O Attic shape! Fair attitude! with brede Of marble men and maidens overwrought, With forest branches and the trodden weed; Thou, silent form, dost tease us out of thought As doth eternity: Cold Pastoral! When old age shall this generation waste Thou shalt remain, in midst of other woe Than ours, a friend to man, to whom thou say'st, "Beauty is truth, truth beauty,"-- that is all Ye know on earth, and all ye need to know.

--KEATS.

VII

It was a lover and his lass With a hey and a ho, and a hey nonino! That o'er the green corn-field did pass In the spring time, the only pretty ring time, When birds do sing hey ding a ding: Sweet lovers love the Spring.

Between the acres of the rye These pretty country folks would lie: This carol they began that hour, How that life was but a flower:

And therefore take the present time With a hey and a ho and a hey nonino! For love is crown 閭 with the prime In spring time, the only pretty ring time, When birds do sing hey ding a ding: Sweet lovers love the Spring.

--SHAKESPEARE.

VIII

Pack, clouds, away, and welcome day, With night we banish sorrow; Sweet air blow soft, mount larks aloft To give my Love good-morrow! Wings from the wind to please her mind Notes from the lark I'll borrow; Bird, prune thy wing, nightingale sing, To give my Love good-morrow; To give my Love good-morrow Notes from them both I'll borrow.

Wake from thy nest, Robin-red-breast, Sing, birds, in every furrow; And from each hill, let music shrill Give my fair Love good-morrow! Blackbird and thrush in every bush, Stare, linnet, and cock-sparrow! You pretty elves, amongst yourselves Sing my fair Love good-morrow; To give my Love good-morrow Sing, birds, in every furrow!

--HEYWOOD.

IX

THE PASSIONATE SHEPHERD TO HIS LOVE

Come live with me and be my Love, And we will all the pleasures prove That hills and valleys, dale and field, And all the craggy mountains yield.

There will we sit upon the rocks And see the shepherds feed their flocks, By shallow rivers, to whose falls Melodious birds sing madrigals.

There will I make thee beds of roses And a thousand fragrant posies, A cap of flowers, and a kirtle Embroider'd all with leaves of myrtle.

A gown made of the finest wool, Which from our pretty lambs we pull, Fair lin 闈 slippers for the cold, With buckles of the purest gold.

A belt of straw and ivy buds With coral clasps and amber studs: And if these pleasures may thee move, Come live with me and be my Love.

Thy silver dishes for thy meat As precious as the gods do eat, Shall on an ivory table be Prepared each day for thee and me.

The shepherd swains shall dance and sing For thy delight each May-morning: If these delights thy mind may move, Then live with me and be my Love.

--MARLOWE.

X

HUNTING SONG

Waken, lords and ladies gay, On the mountain dawns the day; All the jolly chase is here With hawk and horse and hunting-spear; Hounds are in their couples yelling, Hawks are whistling, horns are knelling, Merrily, merrily mingle they, "Waken, lords and ladies gay."

Waken, lords and ladies gay, The mist has left the mountain gray, Springlets in the dawn are steaming, Diamonds on the brake are gleaming; And foresters have busy been To track the buck in thicket green; Now we come to chant our lay "Waken, lords and ladies gay."

Waken, lords and ladies gay, To the greenwood haste away; We can show you where he lies, Fleet of foot and tall of size; We can show the marks he made When 'gainst the oak his antlers fray'd; You shall see him brought to bay; "Waken, lords and ladies gay."

Louder, louder chant the lay Waken, lords and ladies gay! Tell them youth and mirth and glee Run a course as well as we; Time, stern huntsman! who can baulk, Stanch as hound and fleet as hawk; Think of this, and rise with day, Gentle lords and ladies gay!

--SCOTT.

XI

Besides the rivers Arve and Arveiron, which have their sources in the foot of Mont Blanc, five conspicuous torrents rush down its sides; and within a few paces of the Glaciers, the Gentiana Major grows in immense numbers, with its "flowers of loveliest blue."

HYMN

BEFORE SUNRISE, IN THE VALE OF CHAMOUNI

Hast thou a charm to stay the morning-star In his steep course? So long he seems to pause On thy bald awful head, O sovran Blanc! The Arve and Arveiron at thy base Rave ceaselessly; but thou, most awful Form! Risest from forth thy silent sea of pines, How silently! Around thee and above Deep is the air and dark, substantial, black, An ebon mass: methinks thou piercest it, As with a wedge! But when I look again, It is thine own calm home, thy crystal shrine, Thy habitation from eternity! O dread and silent Mount! I gazed upon thee, Till thou, still present to the bodily sense, Didst vanish from my thought: entranced in prayer I worshiped the Invisible alone.

Yet, like some sweet beguiling melody, So sweet, we know not we are listening to it, Thou, the meanwhile, wast blending with my thought, Yea, with my life and life's own secret joy: Till the dilating Soul, enrapt, transfused, Into the mighty vision passing--there As in her natural form, swelled vast to Heaven! Awake, my Soul! not only passive praise Thou owest! not alone these swelling tears, Mute thanks and secret ecstasy! Awake, Voice of sweet song! Awake, my Heart, awake! Green vales and icy cliffs, all join my Hymn.

Thou first and chief, sole sovran of the Vale! O struggling with the darkness all the night, And visited all night by troops of stars, Or when they climb the sky or when they sink; Companion of the morning-star at dawn, Thyself Earth's rosy star, and of the dawn Co-herald: wake, O wake, and utter praise! Who sank thy sunless pillars deep in Earth? Who filled thy countenance with rosy light? Who made thee parent of perpetual streams?

And you, ye five wild torrents fiercely glad! Who called you forth from night and utter death, From dark and icy caverns called you forth, Down those precipitous, black, jagged Rocks, Forever shattered and the same forever?

Who gave you your invulnerable life, Your strength, your speed, your fury, and your joy, Unceasing thunder and eternal foam? And who commanded (and the silence came), Here let the billows stiffen, and have rest?

Ye ice-falls! ye that from the mountain's brow Adown enormous ravines slope amain-- Torrents, methinks, that heard a mighty voice, And stopped at once amid their maddest plunge! Motionless torrents! silent cataracts! Who made you glorious as the gates of Heaven Beneath the keen full moon? Who bade the Sun Clothe you with rainbows? Who, with living flowers Of loveliest blue, spread garlands at your feet?-- God! let the torrents, like a shout of nations, Answer! and let the ice-plains echo, God! God! sing ye meadow-streams with gladsome voice! Ye pine-groves, with your soft and soul-like sounds! And they too have a voice, yon piles of snow, And in their perilous fall shall thunder, God!

Ye living flowers that skirt the eternal frost! Ye wild goats sporting round the eagle's nest! Ye eagles, play-mates of the mountain-storm! Ye lightnings, the dread arrows of the clouds! Ye signs and wonders of the element! Utter forth

God, and fill the hills with praise!

Thou too, hoar Mount! with thy sky-pointing peaks, Oft from whose feet the avalanche, unheard, Shoots downward, glittering through the pure serene Into the depth of clouds that veil thy breast-- Thou too again--stupendous Mountain! thou That as I raise my head, awhile bowed low In adoration, upward from thy base Slow traveling with dim eyes suffused with tears, Solemnly seemest like a vapory cloud, To rise before me--Rise, O ever rise, Rise like a cloud of incense, from the Earth! Thou kingly Spirit throned among the hills, Thou dread ambassador from Earth to Heaven, Great hierarch! tell thou the silent sky, And tell the stars, and tell yon rising sun, Earth, with her thousand voices, praises God.

--COLERIDGE.

XII

JAUN'S SONG FROM THE SPANISH GYPSY

Memory, Tell to me What is fair Past compare In the land of Tubal?

Is it Spring's Lovely things, Blossoms white, Rosy dight? Then it is Pepita.

Summer's crest Red-gold tressed, Corn-flowers peeping under? Idle noons, Lingering moons, Sudden cloud, Lightning's shroud,

Sudden rain, Quick again Smiles where late was thunder? Are all these Made to please? So too is Pepita.

Autumn's prime, Apple-time, Smooth cheek round, Heart all sound?-- Is it this You would kiss? Then it is Pepita.

You can bring No sweet thing, But my mind Still shall find It is my Pepita.

Memory Says to me It is she-- She is fair Past compare In the land of Tubal.

XIII

PABLO'S SONG FROM THE SPANISH GYPSY

Spring comes hither, Buds the rose; Roses wither, Sweet spring goes. Ojala, would she carry me!

Summer soars-- Wide-winged day, White light pours, Flies away. Ojala, would he carry me!

Soft winds blow, Westward born, Onward go Toward the morn. Ojala, would they carry me!

Sweet birds sing O'er the graves, Then take wing O'er the waves. Ojala, would they carry me!

--GEORGE ELIOT.

XIV

MEMORY[5]

[5] This and the following poem appear by special permission of Houghton Mifflin Company, the publishers of Mr. Aldrich's poems.

My mind lets go a thousand things, Like dates of wars and deaths of kings, And yet recalls the very hour-- 'Twas noon by yonder village tower, And on the last blue noon in May-- The wind came briskly up this way, Crisping the brook beside the road; Then, pausing here, set down its load Of pine-scents, and shook listlessly Two petals from that wild-rose-tree.

XV

ENAMOURED ARCHITECT OF AIRY RHYME

Enamoured architect of airy rhyme, Build as thou wilt; heed not what each man says: Good souls, but innocent of dreamer's ways, Will come, and marvel why thou wastest time; Others, beholding how thy turrets climb 'Twixt theirs and heaven, will hate thee all thy days; But most beware of those who come to praise. O Wondersmith, O Worker in sublime And Heaven-sent dreams, let art be all in all; Build as thou wilt, unspoiled by praise or blame, Build as thou wilt, and as thy light is given: Then, if at last the airy structure fall, Dissolve, and vanish--take thyself no shame. They fail, and they alone, who have not striven.

--THOMAS BAILEY ALDRICH.

XVI

LOVE IN THE WINDS[6]

[6] From Along the Trail, by Richard Hovey. Copyright, 1898, by Small, Maynard & Co., Duffield & Co., successors.

When I am standing on a mountain crest, Or hold the tiller in the dashing spray, My love of you leaps foaming in my breast, Shouts with the winds and sweeps to their foray; My heart bounds with the horses of the sea, And plunges in the wild ride of the night Flaunts in the teeth of tempest the large glee That rides out Fate and welcomes gods to fight. Ho, love, I laugh aloud for love of you, Glad that our love is fellow to rough weather,-- No fretful orchid hot-housed from the dew, But hale and hardy as the highland heather, Rejoicing in the wind that stings and thrills, Comrades of ocean, playmate of the hills.

--RICHARD HOVEY.

XVII

CANDLEMAS[7]

[7] By permission of Houghton Mifflin Company.

O hearken, all ye little weeds That lie beneath the snow, (So low, dear hearts, in poverty so low!) The sun hath risen for royal deeds, A valiant wind the vanguard leads; Now quicken ye, lest unborn seeds Before ye rise and blow.

O furry living things, adream On Winter's drowsy breast, (How rest ye there, how softly, safely rest!) Arise and follow where a gleam Of wizard gold unbinds the stream, And all the woodland windings seem With sweet expectance blest.

My birds, come back! the hollow sky Is weary for your note. (Sweet-throat, come back! O liquid, mellow throat!) Ere May's soft minions hereward fly, Shame on ye, laggards, to deny The brooding breast, the sun-bright eye, The tawny, shining coat!

--ALICE BROWN.

Mr. Gilbert Chesterton tells us that the real Robert Browning of literary history arrived with the Dramatic Lyrics. "In Dramatic Lyrics," says Mr. Chesterton, "Browning discovered the one thing that he could really do better than any one else--the dramatic lyric. The form is absolutely original; he had discovered a new field of poetry, and in the center of that field he had found himself." The form is new, but it obeys the fundamental law of lyric poetry, and so in our study belongs to this chapter. The new element which the word "dramatic" suggests makes a new and a somewhat broader demand upon the interpreter; therefore I have chosen this group of Dramatic Lyrics from Browning as the material for your final study of this form:

MY STAR

All that I know Of a certain star Is, it can throw (Like the angled spar) Now a dart of red, Now a dart of blue; Till my friends have said They would fain see, too, My star that dartles the red and the blue! Then it stops like a bird; like a flower, hangs furled: They must solace themselves with the Saturn above it. What matter to me if their star is a world? Mine has opened its soul to me; therefore I love it.

CAVALIER TUNES

MARCHING ALONG

Kentish Sir Byng stood for his King, Bidding the crop-headed Parliament swing. And, pressing a troop unable to stoop And see the rogues flourish and honest folk droop, Marched them along, fifty-score strong, Great-hearted gentlemen, singing this song.

God for King Charles! Pym and such carles To the Devil that prompts 'em their treasonous parles! Cavaliers, up! Lips from the cup, Hands from the pasty, nor bite take nor sup Till you're-- (Chorus) Marching along, fifty-score strong, Great-hearted gentlemen, singing this song.

Hampden to hell, and his obsequies' knell Serve Hazelrig, Fiennes, and young Harry as well! England, good cheer! Rupert is near! Kentish and loyalists, keep we not here, (Chorus) Marching along, fifty-score strong, Great-hearted gentlemen, singing this song?

Then, God for King Charles! Pym and his snarls To the Devil that pricks on such pestilent carles! Hold by the right, you double your might; So, onward to Nottingham, fresh for the fight. (Chorus) March we along, fifty-score strong, Great-hearted gentlemen, singing this song!

GARDEN FANCIES

THE FLOWER'S NAME

Here's the garden she walked across, Arm in my arm, such a short while since. Hark, now I push its wicket, the moss Hinders the hinges and makes them wince! She must have reached this shrub ere she turned, As back with that murmur the wicket swung; For she laid the poor snail, my chance foot spurned, To feed and forget it the leaves among.

Down this side of the gravel walk She went while her robe's edge brushed the box: And here she paused in her gracious talk To point me a moth on the milk-white phlox. Roses, ranged in valiant row, I will never think that she passed you by! She loves you, noble roses, I know; But yonder, see, where the rock-plants lie!

This flower she stopped at, finger on lip, Stooped over, in doubt, as settling its claim; Till she gave me, with pride to make no slip, Its soft meandering Spanish name. What a name! Was it love or praise? Speech half-asleep or song half-awake? I must learn Spanish, one of these days, Only for that slow sweet name's sake.

Roses, if I live and do well, I may bring her, one of these days, To fix you fast with as fine a spell, Fit you each with his Spanish phrase; But do not detain me now; for she lingers There, like sunshine over the ground, And ever I see her soft white fingers Searching after the bud she found.

Flower, you Spaniard, look that you grow not, Stay as you are and be loved forever! Bud, if I kiss you 'tis that you blow not: Mind, the shut pink mouth opens never! For while it pouts, her fingers wrestle, Twinkling the audacious leaves between, Till round they turn and down they nestle-- Is not the dear mark still to be seen?

Where I find her not, beauties vanish; Whither I follow her, beauties flee; Is there no method to tell her in Spanish June's twice June since she breathed it with me? Come, bud, show me the least of her traces, Treasure my lady's lightest footfall! --Ah, you may flout and turn up your faces-- Roses, you are not so fair after all!

--BROWNING.

That "the poet is born, not made," is more and more an undisputed fact in every literary age. But many a birthright of poetic power has been saved from sale for a mess of pottage by a wisely ordered meeting of the young bard, while his gift was still latent, with the masters of lyric expression.

Such an introduction is the object of this study, so far as it can embrace in its aim the ends of both forms of expression,--interpretation and composition. There is no thought of inducing even an aspirant to the poetical purple, much less a Shelley or a Keats or an Alice Brown, through this brief dwelling with their immortal songs; but if this intensive interpretative study of the highest lyric expression does not result in a new sense of word values, a new sensitiveness to the music of the English language, out of which the songs of America must be made, then the study will have failed in its purpose toward you. If from this suggestive analysis of Shelley's "Skylark" you receive no impulse to use words with a new delight in the fitting of sound to sense, a new reverence for their harmonious arrangement to suggest and sustain an atmosphere; if, in short, your vocabulary is not enriched and your choice of words clarified through this study, then your new acquaintance with lyric expression will have been in vain. And, finally, if some one of you at least is not impelled by these excursions into the world of song to use his enriched vocabulary in an attempt to create a bit of lyric description in prose or verse, then the author of this study, and the teacher under whose direction it is made, must admit a failure to reach with the pupil the ultimate aim of such interpretative effort.

Let us make the test. As a final problem of this study I shall ask you to let your emotion find expression--lyric expression--in a bit of prose description. Don't be afraid! Use your vocabulary! Take as a subject: the bit of earth and sky you have secretly worshiped; the bird song or flight which has charmed your day; the memory of some illumined moment; the effect of any one of these lyrics upon you. Don't be afraid! And remember it is to be literature of feeling rather than thought; description, not exposition.

THIRD STUDY

TO DEVELOP THE WHIMSICAL SENSE

Addressing the Gentle Reader in deliciously whimsical vein on the Mission of Humor, Mr. Samuel Arthur Crothers declares: "Were I appointed by the school board to consider the applicants for teachers' certificates, after they had passed the examinations in the arts and sciences, I should subject them to a more rigid test. I should hand each candidate Lamb's essays on 'The Old and New Schoolmaster' and on 'Imperfect Sympathies.' I should make him read them to himself, while I sat by and watched. If his countenance never relaxed, as if he were inwardly saying, 'That's so,' I should withhold the certificate. I should not consider him a fit person to have charge of innocent youth." We can readily see from this extract that we need not go back to the early part of the last century to find material for our test of this sovereign quality, a sense of humor. Mr. Crothers himself, the Charles Lamb of our American Letters to-day, shall furnish our subject-matter. Bring your Gentle Reader, or The Pardoner's Wallet, or the essays collected with the Christmas Sermon, to class to-morrow. If these volumes are not in your personal library, your library is sadly lacking. Read "The Honorable Points of Ignorance," "How to Know the Fallacies," or "Conscience Concerning Witchcraft." If any one of these fails to disclose in you the mental alertness and power of discrimination which their author considers to be requisite characteristics of a true sense of humor, then you are sadly lacking in that coveted quality of mind and heart, and it behooves us to make an attempt to supply these deficiencies.

Can a sense of humor be cultivated, and if it can be cultivated, is it safe to do so? some one asks--some one who has suffered at the hands of a clever jester perhaps. By way of arriving at an answer, let us examine a little further the category of qualities which Mr. Crothers considers requisite to true humor.

We have already noted mental alertness and power of discrimination. There can be no question as to the desirability or feasibility of developing these characteristics, since such development belongs to the fundamental effort of education. But these are but two characteristics of the quality we are considering, and not the distinguishing ones. "Humor," continues the category, "is the frank enjoyment of the imperfect." Now we scent a danger! For if, as Mr. Crothers admits, "artistic sensibility finds satisfaction only in the perfect," and since, as we all admit, artistic sensibility is an end in education devoutly to be desired, then is not a cultivation of the "frank enjoyment of the imperfect," oh dear and gentle humorist, a dangerous indulgence? The conclusive answer comes: "One may have learned to enjoy the sublime, the beautiful, the useful, the orderly, but he has missed something if he has not also learned to enjoy the incongruous, the illusive, and the unexpected." It is a conclusive reply, because we know that it is just as essential to achievement in the finest of the Fine Arts,--the art of living, as in every other form of Art, to recognize that the inrush of discord is for the final issue of harmony; that only through our ability to recognize illusion shall we come to know reality; that only through sensitiveness to the incongruous shall we develop a true sense of the fitness of things; that only frank enjoyment can disarm imperfection and find satisfaction in the perfect. So let us not hesitate to do all we can to cultivate a quality which Thackeray defines as a mixture of love and wit; to which Erasmus ascribes such desirable characteristics as good temper and insight into human nature; and for one grade of which, in addition to all its other qualities, Mr. Crothers claims "that it can proceed only from a mind free from any taint of morbidness."

If then we conclude that it is not only safe, but possible and desirable, to cultivate a sense of humor, how shall we set about it? To answer you, as to one way at least, and that a way of interpretation, Mr. Crothers "is left alive," not only to furnish new material for the exercise of the sense, but to point a gently reminding finger toward the immortal sources of good humor,--

"Chaucer and Cervantes and Montaigne; Shakespeare and Bacon and Fielding and Addison; Goldsmith, Charles Lamb, and Walter Scott, and in our own country, Irving and Dr. Holmes and James Russell Lowell." Whatever period of time your schedule grants to this phase of the work should be dedicated to a closer acquaintance with the flavor and atmosphere of these great-hearted humorists in their most genial moments. Let us also heed Mr. Crothers' warning against the humor of the Dean Swifts which "would be so irresistible were it not bad humor." Let us avoid more intimate acquaintance with the broad variety furnished by the Mark Twains and Mr. Dooleys, which may be legitimately classed as "good humor," but which is so obvious as to be little conducive to that mental alertness and power of discrimination which we aim to acquire through this study. Instead, let us seek the gracious company of William Dean Howells in the whimsical mood he so often induces.

Accepting, then, as a distinguishing characteristic of the humor we desire to cultivate, ability to enjoy the incongruous, the illusive, and the unexpected, let us look to a master maker of these conditions for class-room guidance in this effort. I suppose Mr. Lewis Carroll has done more to develop this distinguishing characteristic than any other contributor to our Letters. So we shall go on an excursion with his Alice into the Wonderland he made for her. If her frank enjoyment and free acceptance of the incongruous and the unexpected does not prove infectious, we must be forever written down among those who could not understand Peter Pan. We shall read and enjoy a chapter or two of Alice together in class, but for suggestive analysis along interpretative lines Heaven forbid that I should lay violent hands on her text. No one can teach you to interpret your Alice save Alice herself. You may walk with her, talk with her, dwindle and grow with her, join her adventures in any way she will permit, but you may not analyze nor dissect her. You may learn to interpret her only by living with her and loving her.

Now Aesop is another matter. However long you may live with him, however much you may love his fables, there is a trick of interpretation to be learned in voicing his philosophy which will develop the whimsical side of your sense of humor and counteract the insistent moral tone attached to every fable.

SUGGESTIVE ANALYSIS

The danger in handling a fable does not lie, as the interpreter seems so often to think, in adopting too serious a tone. All the literature of pure fancy, from the humorous essays of Bacon through the Arabian Nights to the nonsensical rhymes of Lear, must be treated with great gravity of tone and temper by the interpreter. It is not levity, but only whimsicality of temperament, I demand from one who would read from this particular lore to me. I want my whimsical friend to interpret my Chaucer and Crothers, Peter Pan and the Pied Piper, Hans Christian Andersen, Carroll, and Lear, and all the rest of the genial host who minister to my most precious sense of nonsense. And, perhaps, most of all, it is he (the whimsical friend) who must read fables to me, for a fable, the dictionary tells us, is "a story in which, by the imagined dealings of men with animals or mere things, or by the supposed doings of these alone, useful lessons are taught." Now a moral "rubbed in" is like an overdose of certain kinds of medicine, where a little cures, too much kills. It is the presence of the lesson which the whimsical tone alone can offset. The whimsical tone never falls into the monotone. Whimsicality always seeks variety of emphasis and movement. Let us apply this to the reading of the fable called

THE CROW AND THE PITCHER

A crow, half dead with thirst, came upon a pitcher which had once been full of water; but when the crow put his beak into the mouth of the pitcher he found that only very little water was left in it, and that he could not reach far enough down to get at it. He tried, and he tried, but at last had to give up in despair. Then a thought came to him, and he took a pebble and dropped it into the pitcher. Then he took another pebble and dropped it into the pitcher. Then he took another pebble and dropped that into the pitcher. Then he took another pebble and dropped that into the pitcher. Then he took another pebble and dropped that into the pitcher. Then he took another pebble and dropped that into the pitcher. At last, at last, he saw the water mount up near him; and after casting in a few more pebbles he was able to quench his thirst and save his life.

Little by little does the trick.

How shall we avoid the monotony of the lines beginning "Then he took another pebble and dropped it into the pitcher"? Note that this line is followed by one in which but two words are changed, and then by a line with but one change, and then by three lines with no change at all. Our only hope lies in a variation of emphasis and movement--a whimsical variation. Try it! Give "another" the particular stress in reading the first of these lines. Pause at the close of the line as if to study the effect of the pebble. In the next line "that," of course, takes the emphasis. Pause before the word and give it a salient stress. The movement of the voice through these two lines has been deliberate. On the next line hasten it a little, and make the pause at the close of the line shorter. With the fourth line let the tone settle down to work. Give each of the first five words equal stress. With the fifth and last line let us feel that you may "go on forever," and surprise us with a very short pause and a joyful stress upon "at last, at last," and don't fail to let the enthusiasm of your tone give us the full sense of the relief which comes with the mounting of the water, and the delight in the conclusion--"he was able to quench his thirst and save his life." And now, most whimsically, let us voice the moral, "Little by little does the trick."

SELECTIONS FOR INTERPRETATION

THE LION AND THE MOUSE

Once when a lion was asleep a little mouse began running up and down upon him; this soon wakened the lion, who placed his huge paw upon him, and opened his big jaws to swallow him. "Pardon, O King," cried the little mouse; "forgive me this time. I shall never forget it; who knows but what I may be able to do you a turn some of these days?" The lion was so tickled at the idea of the mouse being able to help him, that he lifted up his paw and let him go. Some time after the lion was caught in a trap, and the hunters, who desired to carry him alive to the king, tied him to a tree while they went in search of a wagon to carry him on. Just then the little mouse happened to pass by, and seeing the sad plight in which the lion was, went up to him and soon gnawed away the ropes that bound the king of the beasts. "Was I not right?" said the little mouse.

Little friends may prove great friends.

THE WIND AND THE SUN

The wind and the sun were disputing which was the stronger. Suddenly they saw a traveler coming down the road, and the sun said: "I see a way to decide our dispute. Whichever of us can cause that traveler to take off his cloak shall be regarded as the stronger. You begin." So the sun retired behind a cloud, and the wind began to blow as hard as he could upon the traveler. But the harder he blew the more closely did the traveler wrap his cloak round him, till at last the wind had to give up in despair. Then the sun came out and shone in all his glory upon the traveler, who soon found it too hot to walk with his cloak on.

Kindness effects more than severity.

And, now, here is Alice herself to play with a little. Go fearlessly into her Wonderland and let her teach you "how to meet the illusive, the incongruous, and the unexpected." Let her minister to your ability to enjoy the imperfect. Let her develop your sense of humor. If she cannot do so no one can.

DOWN THE RABBIT-HOLE[8]

[8] These following selections are taken from Harper & Brothers' edition of Alice in Wonderland and Alice Through the Looking-Glass.

Alice was beginning to get very tired of sitting by her sister on the bank, and of having nothing to do; once or twice she had peeped into the book her sister was reading, but it had no pictures or conversations in it, "and what is the use of a book," thought Alice, "without pictures or conversations?"

So she was considering in her own mind (as well as she could, for the hot day made her feel very sleepy and stupid) whether the pleasure of making a daisy-chain would be worth the trouble of getting up and picking the daisies, when suddenly a White Rabbit with pink eyes ran close by her.

There was nothing so very remarkable in that; nor did Alice think it so very much out of the way to hear the Rabbit say to itself, "Oh dear! Oh dear! I shall be too late!" (when she thought it over afterward, it occurred to her that she ought to have wondered at this, but at the time it all seemed quite natural); but when the Rabbit actually took a watch out of its waistcoat-pocket, and looked at it, and then hurried on, Alice started to her feet, for it flashed across her mind that she had never before seen a rabbit with either a waistcoat-pocket, or a watch to take out of it, and, burning with curiosity, she ran across the field after it, and fortunately was just in time to see it pop down a large rabbit-hole under the hedge.

In another moment down went Alice after it, never once considering how in the world she was to get out again.

The rabbit-hole went straight on like a tunnel for some way, and then dipped suddenly down--so suddenly that Alice had not a moment to think about stopping herself before she found herself falling down a very steep well.

Either the well was very deep, or she fell very slowly, for she had plenty of time as she went down to look about her, and to wonder what was going to happen next. First, she tried to look down and make out what she was coming to, but it was too dark to see anything; then she looked at the sides of the well, and noticed that they were filled with cupboards and bookshelves; here and there she saw maps and pictures hung upon pegs. She took down a jar from one of the shelves as she passed; it was labeled "ORANGE MARMALADE," but to her great disappointment it was empty. She did not like to drop the jar for fear of killing somebody, so managed to put it into one of the cupboards as she fell past it.

"Well!" thought Alice to herself. "After such a fall as this, I shall think nothing of tumbling down-stairs! How brave they'll all think me at home! Why, I wouldn't say anything about it, even if I fell off the top of the house!" (Which was very likely true.)

Down, down, down. Would the fall never come to an end? "I wonder how many miles I've fallen by this time?" she said, aloud. "I must be getting somewhere near the center of the earth. Let me see: that would be four thousand miles down, I think--" (for, you see, Alice had learned several things of this sort in her lessons in the school-room, and though this was not a very good opportunity for showing off her knowledge, as there was no one to listen to her, still it was good practice to say it over) "--yes, that's about the right distance--but then I wonder what Latitude or Longitude I've got to?" (Alice had no idea what Latitude was, or Longitude either, but thought they were nice, grand words to say.)

Presently she began again. "I wonder if I shall fall right through the earth? How funny it'll seem to come out among the people that walk with their heads downward! The Antipathies, I think--" (she was rather glad there was no one listening this time, as it didn't sound at all the right word) "--but I shall have to ask them what the name of the country is, you know. 'Please, ma'am, is this New Zealand or Australia?'" (and she tried to courtesy as she spoke-- fancy courtesying as you're falling through the air! Do you think you could manage it?) "And what an ignorant little girl she'll think me! No, it'll never do to ask; perhaps I shall see it written up somewhere."

Down, down, down. There was nothing else to do, so Alice soon began talking again. "Dinah'll miss me very much to-night, I should think!" (Dinah was the cat.) "I hope they'll remember her saucer of milk at tea-time. Dinah, my dear, I wish you were down here with me! There are no mice in the air, I'm afraid, but you might catch a bat, and that's very like a mouse, you know. But do cats eat bats, I wonder?" And here Alice began to get rather sleepy, and went on saying to herself, in a dreamy sort of way, "Do cats eat bats? Do cats eat bats?" and sometimes, "Do bats eat cats?" for, you see, as she couldn't answer either question, it didn't much matter which way she put it. She felt that she was dozing off, and had just begun to dream that she was walking hand in hand with Dinah, and saying to her very earnestly, "Now, Dinah, tell me the truth: did you ever eat a bat?" when suddenly, thump! thump! down she came upon a heap of dry leaves, and the fall was over.

Alice was not a bit hurt, and she jumped up on her feet in a moment. She looked up, but it was all dark overhead; before her was another long passage, and the White Rabbit was still in sight, hurrying down it. There was not a moment to be lost; away went Alice like the wind, and was just in time to hear it say, as it turned a corner, "Oh my ears and whiskers, how late it's getting!" She was close behind it when she turned the corner, but the Rabbit was no longer to be seen; she found herself in a long, low hall, which was lit up by a row of lamps hanging from the roof.

There were doors all round the hall, but they were all locked; and when Alice had been all the way down one side and up the other, trying every door, she walked sadly down the middle, wondering how she was ever to get out again.

Suddenly she came upon a little three-legged table, all made of solid glass; there was nothing on it except a tiny golden key, and Alice's first thought was that it might belong to one of the doors of the hall; but, alas! either the locks were too large or the key was too small, but at any rate it would not open any of them. However, the second time round she came upon a low curtain she had not noticed before, and behind it was a little door about fifteen inches high. She tried the little golden key in the lock, and to her great delight it fitted!

Alice opened the door and found that it led into a small passage, not much larger than a rat-hole. She knelt down and looked along the passage into the loveliest garden you ever saw. How she longed to get out of that dark hall, and wander about among those beds of bright flowers and those cool fountains, but she could not even get her head through the doorway! "And even if my head would go through," thought poor Alice, "it would be of very little use without my shoulders. Oh, how I wish I could shut up like a telescope! I think I could, if I only knew how to begin." For, you see, so many out-of-the-way things had happened lately that Alice had begun to think that very few things indeed were really impossible.

There seemed to be no use in waiting by the little door, so she went back to the table, half hoping she might find another key on it, or, at any rate, a book of rules for shutting people up like telescopes. This time she found a little bottle on it ("which certainly was not here before," said Alice), and round its neck a paper label, with the words "DRINK ME" beautifully printed on it in large letters.

It was all very well to say "Drink me," but the wise little Alice was not going to do that in a hurry. "No, I'll look first," she said, "and see whether it's marked 'poison' or not"; for she had read several nice little histories about children who had got burned, and eaten up by wild beasts, and many other unpleasant things, all because they would not remember the simple rules their friends had taught them: such as, that a red-hot poker will burn you if you hold it too long; and that, if you cut your finger very deeply with a knife, it usually bleeds; and she had never forgotten that, if you drink much from a bottle marked "poison," it is almost certain to disagree with you, sooner or later.

However, this bottle was not marked "poison," so Alice ventured to taste it, and, finding it very nice (it had, in fact, a sort of mixed flavor of cherry-tart, custard, pineapple, roast turkey, toffee, and hot buttered toast), she very soon finished it off.

* * * * *

"What a curious feeling!" said Alice. "I must be shutting up like a telescope."

And so it was, indeed: she was now only ten inches high, and her face brightened up at the thought that she was now the right size for going through the little door into that lovely garden. First, however, she waited for a few minutes to see if she was going to shrink any further: she felt a little nervous about this, "for it might end, you know," said Alice, "in my going out altogether, like a candle. I wonder what I should be like then?" And she tried to fancy what the flame of a candle is like after it is blown out, for she could not remember ever having seen such a thing.

After a while, finding that nothing more happened, she decided to go into the garden at once, but, alas for poor Alice! when she got to the door she found she had forgotten the little golden key, and when she went back to the table for it she found she could not possibly reach it. She could see it quite plainly through the glass, and she tried her best to climb up one of the table-legs, but it was too slippery; and when she had tired herself out with trying, the poor little thing sat down and cried.

"Come, there's no use in crying like that!" said Alice to herself, rather sharply. "I advise you to leave off this minute!" She generally gave herself very good advice (though she very seldom followed it), and sometimes she scolded herself so severely as to bring tears in her eyes; and once she remembered trying to box her own ears for having cheated herself in a game of croquet she was playing against herself, for this curious child was very fond of pretending to be two people. "But it's no use now," thought poor Alice, "to pretend to be two people! Why, there's hardly enough of me left to make one respectable person!"

Soon her eye fell on a little glass box that was lying under the table. She opened it, and found in it a very small cake, on which the words "EAT ME" were beautifully marked in currants. "Well, I'll eat it," said Alice, "and if it makes me larger I can reach the key, and if it makes me smaller I can creep under the door; so, either way, I'll get into the garden, and I don't care which happens!"

She ate a little bit and said anxiously to herself, "Which way? Which way?" holding her hand on the top of her head to feel which way it was growing, and she was quite surprised to find that she remained the same size. To be sure, this generally happens when one eats cake, but Alice had got so much into the way of expecting nothing but out-of-the-way things to happen that it seemed quite dull and stupid for life to go on in the common way.

So she set to work, and very soon finished off the cake.

* * * * *

THE POOL OF TEARS

"Curiouser and curiouser!" cried Alice (she was so much surprised that for the moment she quite forgot how to speak good English); "now I'm opening out like the largest telescope that ever was! Good-by, feet!" (for when she looked down at her feet they seemed to be almost out of sight, they were getting so far off). "Oh, my poor little feet, I wonder who will put on your shoes and stockings for you now, dears? I'm sure I sha'n't be able! I shall be a great deal too far off to trouble myself about you: you must manage the best way you can--but I must be kind to them," thought Alice, "or perhaps they won't walk the way I want to go! Let me see; I'll give them a new pair of boots every Christmas."

And she went on planning to herself how she would manage it. "They must go by the carrier," she thought; "and how funny it'll seem, sending presents to one's own feet! And how odd the directions will look!--

Alice's Right Foot, Esq. Hearthrug, near the Fender (with Alice's love).

Oh dear, what nonsense I'm talking!"

Just then her head struck against the roof of the hall--in fact she was now more than nine feet high--and she at once took up the little golden key and hurried off to the garden door.

Poor Alice! It was as much as she could do, lying down on one side, to look through into the garden with one eye, but to get through was more hopeless than ever. She sat down and began to cry again.

"You ought to be ashamed of yourself," said Alice--"a great girl like you" (she might well say this), "to go on crying in this way! Stop this moment, I tell you!" But she went on all the same, shedding gallons of tears, until there was a large pool all round her, about four inches deep and reaching half down the hall.

After a time she heard a little pattering of feet in the distance, and she hastily dried her eyes to see what was coming. It was the White Rabbit returning, splendidly dressed, with a pair of white kid gloves in one hand and a large fan in the other. He came trotting along in a great hurry, muttering to himself as he came, "Oh! the Duchess, the Duchess! Oh! won't she be savage if I've kept her waiting!" Alice felt so desperate that she was ready to ask help of any one; so, when the Rabbit came near her, she began, in a low, timid voice, "If you please, sir--" The Rabbit started violently, dropped the white kid gloves and the fan, and scurried away into the darkness as hard as he could go.

Alice took up the fan and gloves, and, as the hall was very hot, she kept fanning herself all the time she went on talking: "Dear, dear! How queer everything is to-day! And yesterday things went on just as usual. I wonder if I've been changed in the night? Let me think: was I the same when I got up this morning? I almost think I can remember feeling a little different. But if I'm not the same, the next question is, Who in the world am I? Ah, that's the great puzzle!" And she began thinking over all the children she knew that were of the same age as herself, to see if she could have been changed for any of them.

"I'm sure I'm not Ada," she said, "for her hair goes in such long ringlets, and mine doesn't go in ringlets at all; and I'm sure I can't be Mabel, for I know all sorts of things, and she, oh! she knows such a very little! Besides, she's she and I'm I, and--oh dear, how puzzling it all is! I'll try if I know all the things I used to know. Let me see: four times five is twelve, and four times six is thirteen, and four times seven is--oh dear! I shall never get to twenty at that rate! However, the Multiplication Table doesn't signify: let's try Geography. London is the capital of Paris, and Paris is the capital of Rome, and Rome--no, that's all wrong, I'm certain! I must have been changed for Mabel! I'll try and say 'How doth the little--'" and she crossed her hands on her lap as if she were saying lessons, and began to repeat it, but her voice sounded hoarse and strange, and the words did not come the same as they used to do:

How doth the little crocodile Improve his shining tail, And pour the waters of the Nile On every golden scale!

How cheerfully he seems to grin, How neatly spread his claws, And welcomes little fishes in With gently smiling jaws!

"I'm sure those are not the right words," said poor Alice, and her eyes filled with tears again as she went on: "I must be Mabel, after all, and I shall have to go and live in that poky little house, and have next to no toys to play with, and oh! ever so many lessons to learn! No, I've made up my mind about it; if I'm Mabel, I'll stay down here! It'll be no use their putting their heads down and saying, 'Come up again, dear!' I shall only look up and say, 'Who am I, then? Tell me that first, and then, if I like being that person, I'll come up; if not, I'll stay down here till I'm somebody else.' But, oh dear!" cried Alice, with a sudden burst of tears, "I do wish they would put their heads down! I am so very tired of being all alone here!"

As she said this she looked down at her hands, and was surprised to see that she had put on one of the Rabbit's little white kid gloves while she was talking. "How can I have done that?" she thought. "I must be growing small again." She got up and went to the table to measure herself by it, and found that, as nearly as she could guess, she was now about two feet high, and was going on shrinking rapidly. She soon found out that the cause of this was the fan she was holding, and she dropped it hastily, just in time to avoid shrinking away altogether.

"That was a narrow escape!" said Alice, a good deal frightened at the sudden change, but very glad to find herself still in existence; "and now for the garden!" and she ran with all speed back to the little door; but, alas! the little door was shut again, and the little golden key was lying on the glass table as before, "and things are worse than ever," thought the poor child, "for I never was so small as this before--never! And I declare it's too bad, that it is!"

As she said these words her foot slipped, and in another moment, splash! she was up to her chin in salt water. Her first idea was that she had somehow fallen into the sea, "and in that case I can go back by railway," she said to herself. (Alice had been to the seaside once in her life, and had come to the general conclusion that wherever you go to on the English coast you find a number of bathing-machines in the sea, some children digging in the sand with wooden spades, then a row of lodging-houses, and behind them a railway station.) However, she soon made out that she was in the pool of tears which she had wept when she was nine feet high.

"I wish I hadn't cried so much!" said Alice, as she swam about, trying to find her way out. "I shall be punished for it now, I suppose, by being drowned in my own tears! That will be a queer thing, to be sure! However, everything is queer to-day."

Just then she heard something splashing about in the pool a little way off, and she swam nearer to make out what it was. At first she thought it must be a walrus or hippopotamus, but then she remembered how small she was now, and she soon made out that it was only a mouse that had slipped in like herself.

"Would it be of any use, now," thought Alice, "to speak to this mouse? Everything is so out-of-the-way down here that I should think very likely it can talk; at any rate, there's no harm in trying." So she began: "O Mouse, do you know the way out of this pool? I am very tired of swimming about here, O Mouse!" (Alice thought this must be the right way of speaking to a mouse. She had never done such a thing before, but she remembered having seen in her brother's Latin Grammar, "A mouse--of a mouse--to a mouse--a mouse--O mouse!") The Mouse looked at her rather inquisitively, and seemed to her to wink with one of its little eyes, but it said nothing.

"Perhaps it doesn't understand English," thought Alice; "I dare say it's a

French mouse, come over with William the Conqueror." (For with all her knowledge of history, Alice had no very clear notion how long ago anything had happened.) So she began again: "Ou est ma chatte?" which was the first sentence in her French lesson-book. The Mouse gave a sudden leap out of the water, and seemed to quiver all over with fright. "Oh, I beg your pardon!" cried Alice, hastily, afraid that she had hurt the poor animal's feelings. "I quite forgot you didn't like cats."

"Not like cats!" cried the Mouse, in a shrill, passionate voice. "Would you like cats if you were me?"

"Well, perhaps not," said Alice, in a soothing tone. "Don't be angry about it. And yet I wish I could show you our cat Dinah: I think you'd take a fancy to cats if you could only see her. She is such a dear, quiet thing," Alice went on, half to herself, as she swam lazily about in the pool, "and she sits purring so nicely by the fire, licking her paws and washing her face--and she is such a nice soft thing to nurse--and she's such a capital one for catching mice--oh, I beg your pardon!" cried Alice again, for this time the Mouse was bristling all over, and she felt certain it must be really offended. "We won't talk about her any more, if you'd rather not."

"We, indeed!" cried the Mouse, who was trembling down to the end of his tail. "As if I would talk on such a subject! Our family always hated cats--nasty, low, vulgar things! Don't let me hear the name again!"

"I won't, indeed!" said Alice, in a great hurry to change the subject of conversation. "Are you--are you fond--of--of dogs?" The Mouse did not answer, so Alice went on eagerly: "There is such a nice little dog near our house I should like to show you! A little bright-eyed terrier, you know, with oh, such long, curly brown hair! And it'll fetch things when you throw them, and it'll sit up and beg for its dinner, and all sorts of things--I can't remember half of them--and it belongs to a farmer, you know, and he says it's so useful it's worth a hundred pounds! He says it kills all the rats and--oh dear!" cried Alice in a sorrowful tone, "I'm afraid I've offended it again!" For the Mouse was swimming away from her as hard as it could go, and making quite a commotion in the pool as it went.

So she called softly after it, "Mouse dear! Do come back again, and we won't talk about cats, or dogs either, if you don't like them!" When the Mouse heard this, it turned round and swam slowly back to her. Its face was quite pale (with passion, Alice thought), and it said in a low, trembling voice, "Let us get to the shore, and then I'll tell you my history, and you'll understand why it is I hate cats and dogs."

It was high time to go, for the pool was getting quite crowded with the birds and animals that had fallen into it: there were a Duck and a Dodo, a Lory and an Eaglet, and several other curious creatures. Alice led the way, and the whole party swam to the shore.

THE WALRUS AND THE CARPENTER

The sun was shining on the sea, Shining with all his might; He did his very best to make The billows smooth and bright-- And this was odd, because it was The middle of the night.

The moon was shining sulkily, Because she thought the sun Had got no business to be there After the day was done-- "It's very rude of him," she said, "To come and spoil the fun!"

The sea was wet as wet could be, The sands were dry as dry. You could not see a cloud, because No cloud was in the sky; No birds were flying overhead-- There were no birds to fly.

The Walrus and the Carpenter Were walking close at hand; They wept like anything to see Such quantities of sand-- "If this were only cleared away," They said, "it would be grand!"

"If seven maids with seven mops Swept it for half a year, Do you suppose," the Walrus said, "That they could get it clear?" "I doubt it," said the Carpenter, And shed a bitter tear.

"O Oysters, come and walk with us!" The Walrus did beseech. "A pleasant walk, a pleasant talk, Along the briny beach; We cannot do with more than four, To give a hand to each."

The eldest Oyster looked at him, But never a word he said; The eldest Oyster winked his eye, And shook his heavy head-- Meaning to say he did not choose To leave the oyster-bed.

But four young Oysters hurried up, All eager for the treat; Their coats were brushed, their faces washed, Their shoes were clean and neat-- And this was odd, because, you know, They hadn't any feet.

Four other Oysters followed them, And yet another four; And thick and fast they came at last, And more, and more, and more-- All hopping through the frothy waves, And scrambling to the shore.

The Walrus and the Carpenter Walked on a mile or so, And then they rested on a rock Conveniently low-- And all the little Oysters stood And waited in a row.

"The time has come," the Walrus said, "To talk of many things: Of shoes-- and ships--and sealing-wax-- Of cabbages--and kings-- And why the sea is boiling hot-- And whether pigs have wings."

"But wait a bit," the Oysters cried, "Before we have our chat; For some of us are out of breath, And all of us are fat!" "No hurry!" said the Carpenter. They thanked him much for that.

"A loaf of bread," the Walrus said, "Is what we chiefly need; Pepper and vinegar besides Are very good indeed-- Now, if you're ready, Oysters dear, We can begin to feed."

"But not on us!" the Oysters cried, Turning a little blue. "After such kindness, that would be A dismal thing to do!" "The night is fine," the Walrus said. "Do you admire the view?

"It was so kind of you to come! And you are very nice!" The Carpenter said nothing but, "Cut us another slice. I wish you were not quite so deaf-- I've had to ask you twice!"

"It seems a shame," the Walrus said, "To play them such a trick. After we've brought them out so far, And made them trot so quick!" The Carpenter said nothing but, "The butter's spread too thick!"

"I weep for you," the Walrus said; "I deeply sympathize." With sobs and tears he sorted out Those of the largest size, Holding his pocket-handkerchief Before his streaming eyes.

"O Oysters," said the Carpenter, "You've had a pleasant run! Shall we be trotting home again?" But answer came there none-- And this was scarcely odd, because They'd eaten every one.

We must not deny to humor and fancy the opportunity for creative effort offered to other faculties in our previous studies. What form shall the effort take: fable, fairy tale, a whimsical play of fancy in essay, or merely a nonsense rhyme? I think we must bar the limerick from our serious creative efforts in the study. You may engage as a class in an extemporaneous contest in the making of this infectious form of verse if you like.

Meanwhile, there is still another class-room test of humor which should be made,--the test of the clever anecdote. There is nothing which so effectually discloses the quality of your sense of humor as your attitude toward so-called funny stories. Judgment in such a case will rest upon three points: What you think is "funny" enough to tell; when you judge it "apropos" to tell; and the manner of the telling. Three warnings are in order at this point. If you find that you must preface your anecdote with the question too often heard, "Do you think you can stand this story?--it really is clever," in the name of clean humor, don't tell it! If you find you must introduce your anecdote with the remark, "Apropos of nothing," or "This is not apropos, but"--in the name of "sulphitic" humor, don't tell it; finally, if you don't know how to tell it, in the name of any and all humor, don't tell it.

With these cautions in mind, I shall ask you to bring to class to-morrow your best three "funny stories." Conflicting choice is not likely to have appropriated all three of your favorite anecdotes. Should you find that it has done so, never mind. Your taste, though it coincides with another's, can be quite as well questioned or commended; and the manner of your telling will be subjected to trial by comparison, which, if not always comfortable, is always helpful (when met in the right spirit).

Remember, the serious creative work you are to produce is to take the form of a fable, fairy story, or humorous essay.

FOURTH STUDY

TO DEVELOP IMAGINATIVE VIGOR

In one of the great manufacturing towns of the Northwest there are some twenty-five thousand girls employed in factories. The city permits conditions of work hostile to the physical life of these girls. Civic reform is trying to control these conditions. In time it doubtless will succeed in doing so; meanwhile it makes efforts in other directions. It establishes working girls' clubs. A class in literature in one of these clubs enlisted the services of a comprehending young teacher, who kept the girls interested for more than two years. A little girl from a bag factory entered this class. She came to every meeting of the first year. She did not join in the discussions nor ask questions nor evince unusual intelligence or enjoyment, but she came every night. The class began its second year. The little girl from the bag factory was the first to enroll. The teacher could not cover the surprise in her question, "Are you coming into the class again?" The girl's breathless "Oh yes" sent her to investigate the case. She went to the factory. She found the child standing at a bench folding bags. Eight hours a day she folded bags. A swing back on her right foot with the stuff of which the bag was made grasped in her hands--a swing forward, and her hands brought the edges of the stuff together evenly. Over and over a thousand times the single motion repeated made up the girl's day. "It used to make me tired," she said, simply. "But it doesn't any more?" "No, because now I forget what I am doing sometimes. I have my book, you see. They let me fasten it here." There it was--a paper copy of Shelley's poems. The print was good; the teacher had seen to that. She had observed that factory girls' eyes are not always very strong. The book was fastened to the front of the desk. The child could catch a line from time to time without interrupting her bag-folding. "But I know most of the poems we have studied in class by heart." So she had to recall but a line, and then off she would go through the windows of the stifling factory into the open fields on the wings of her imagination. She was a swift, sure, little workman; her eye watched the stuff before her and measured it truly; her hands obeyed her eye, did her work efficiently, and "kept her job." But the eye of her imagination had been opened in the literature class and kept her soul alive in spite "of her job." This is a true story. It has significance for you and me.

If through the use of her imagination a little factory girl can escape from the monotony of bag-folding, and find freedom and joy in the lyric world Shelley has created, what limit need be set to our emancipation through the development of this faculty?

But emancipation is but one result of such development. Listen to David as he stands with his harp before the King in Browning's story of Saul. Already his song has released the monarch from the depths of his great despair, but now comes the boy's cry:

What spell or what charm (For, awhile there was trouble within me) what next should I urge To sustain him where song had restored him?... Then fancies grew rife Which had come long ago on the pasture, when round me the sheep Fed in silence--above, the one eagle wheeled slow as in sleep; And I lay in my hollow and mused on the world that might lie 'Neath his ken, though I saw but the strip 'twixt the hill and the sky: And I laughed--"Since my days are ordained to be passed with my flocks, Let me people at least, with my fancies, the plains and the rocks, Dream the life I am never to mix with, and image the show Of mankind as they live in those fashions I hardly shall know! Schemes of life, its best rules and right uses, the courage that gains, And the prudence that keeps what men strive for." And now those old trains Of vague thought came again; I grew surer; so, once more the string Of my harp made response to my spirit....

So the imagination of the young shepherd boy had not only disregarded the limits of his actual environment and escaped in fancy to the great world beyond, but so vividly had he realized that world through his imagination that his sympathies had been made broad to comprehend a monarch's need and his song potent to meet it. Experience alone gives comprehension. We are prone to think that experience is limited by our actual horizon. We need to know that experience has no limit save that which is set by the limit of our imaginative insight. No door of life is closed to the imaginative mind and heart. The world is its playground to wander in at will. Experience, and thorough experience, comprehension of life is at the command of imagination.

Life can be intelligently apprehended on the material plane through trained senses. Life can be vividly realized on the spirit's plane only through a trained imagination. It is only vivid realization of life at every point which makes it worth living. You may see the lark long after he is lost to my duller eye in our common sky, you may hear the song when my less keen ear no longer catches a faintest thread of melody; but unless the eye and ear of your imagination match mine you shall not vividly realize flight or song, and so I shall follow both long after they are lost to you. Your skylark will pass with the moment of his rapturous song-flight, while mine shall remain forever a spirit of joy to be recalled at will for my spirit's refreshing.

Looking then upon imagination as a key to that comprehension of life which clarifies and constitutes its worth, let us eagerly enter upon the cultivation of such power. We have left this question of imaginative development as a definite exercise to a fifth place in our interpretative study, not because it is less vital to effective expression than the first four subjects we have considered, but because balanced expression is our aim, and imagination once given free play may easily impair that harmonious development of all our faculties which makes for balance in expression. Of course there is no phase of the study of interpretation which, when rightly conducted, does not indirectly or directly involve the training of the imagination. On the other hand, training of the imagination wisely conducted may comprehend and carry on development along all other lines of evolution in expression. A sensitive imagination trained and controlled to its highest power of apprehension must make for sympathy and intelligence in thought and feeling, keep humor sane, and give direction to purpose. But imaginative vigor set free to the uses of thought and emotion already disciplined, to conscious purpose and to good humor, becomes a safe master of expressive living.

The material through which we are to exercise the imagination and develop imaginative vigor is the narrative form of discourse. Narration is successful when it records or has the effect of recording actual experience. A story (according to the authority we so often invoke,--Mr. Gardiner), "whether it be as simple as those of the Book of Genesis or as complex as Mr. James or Mr. Meredith, must carry the effect of the concreteness, and, as it were, the solidity of life." The plot, the characters, the setting of a story which is to live, must have the vividness of real experience. This does not mean that the creator of the story must have actually experienced the plot, the people, and the pictures which together make up his tale--they may be the product of actual experience or of imagination--but it does mean that while he is putting these elements together and creating his narrative he must realize as though it were actual experience the incident of his plot with the characters and in the atmosphere of his creation. Such realization can only come through vivid imagination.

Exactly the same demand is made upon the imagination of the interpreter. When you retell the tale of a master creator of stories your interpretation will be convincing, exactly as was his creation,--through the lucid play of a vivid imagination. You must make me feel that I am in the presence of incidents, characters, pictures which you yourself have experienced. Nay, more, you must make me feel that I myself am actually meeting these people, seeing these pictures, taking part in these incidents, as you relive for me in imagination at the moment of your interpretation the tale you are retelling to me.

SUGGESTIVE ANALYSIS

We shall use for suggestive analysis in this study not a complete specimen of narration, but several examples illustrating two of the three elements necessary to the personnel of a good story. These three recognized elements are the setting or situation which the pictures compose, the atmosphere which the characters create, and the plot or the action in which the characters engage. We shall leave the question of the plot to class work upon the selections from epic poetry to be considered later in this study.

Suppose we test our imaginations in the analysis of a situation or setting before we attempt a character study. Remember the situation is to be realized through imagination as though it were actual experience. It is to be recreated. Give your imagination full play in this opening chapter of George Eliot's Mill on the Floss. Let us read the first sentence:

A wide plain, where the broadening Floss hurries on between its green banks to the sea, and the loving tide, rushing to meet it, checks its passage with an impetuous embrace.

Can you see and feel the elements of this picture! You have never experienced a tide river? Never mind! There is enough in the picture which is familiar to your actual senses through experience to brace your imagination for a grasp of the unfamiliar elements. The wide plain, the river hurrying between green banks--no apperceptive background fails thus far in the picture. What do we mean by apperceptive background? Let us investigate for a moment the psychology involved in the art of "making pictures." Let us get back of this word-picture. Rather let us stay this side of it. Look at the page before you not with the inner eye of your imagination, but with the outer eye--the eye which is merely the organ of the sense of sight. Use your eye as a physical sense only. What does your eye carry to your mind when you look at this page? "Black letters grouped into words on a white surface." Did you get all these qualities at once? Yes, because you have seen other printed pages. Can you wipe out of your mind your knowledge of paper, print, and words? Can you imagine looking on such a page as this for the first time-- perceiving it for the first time? If you can do this you will arrive at an understanding of apperceptive background through its elimination. You will realize, that all that is in the back of your mind, stored there by its previous acquaintance with other printed pages, makes up the apperceptive background by which you get a conception of this page. That conception comes first through your physical sense of sight. You may perceive also through touch, through feeling, for instance, the quality of paper. But all that you perceive in this initial process,--the stimulus which comes through the physical senses, yields little to the complete conception as compared with the yield of your so-called mental senses. It is when you have fully apperceived the object that your conception is complete. It is when you have brought to bear upon this page (still looked upon, remember, merely as a printed page regardless of the matter behind the print) all your previous knowledge,--it is when you have observed that the paper is of good quality, that the page is closely set, that the print is excellent, that the margin is wide,--it is when you have compared it in memory with other pages in other books,--it is when you have not only perceived but apperceived it that you have really gained a conception of it. Of course, if you are a type-setter, or a proof-reader, or a printer, or an editor, or one connected with book-making in any least or last capacity, you will see a printed page quite lost to me, because your apperceptive background will outmatch mine as to paper, print, margin, and type. Good! I yield to you from type-setter to editor! But I challenge you to another contest over the same page. Match with me now conceptions gained from another view of this same printed matter. Forget now type, paper, margins, and words--yes, forget the words as printed words--look back of them with me. What do you see now on the page? Still words? Look behind them at the pictures! Now, what do you see? "A wide plain, a river, green banks, the sea!" Yes, but I see more than that! And you do, too? "The river flows between green banks?" You have missed a point. How does she flow? Ah, yes, "She hurries on." Where? "To the sea!" Yes! And what meets her? "The tide!" Yes, the loving tide meets her! But how? "Rushing, he checks her passage in an impetuous embrace!" "You see all this!" you say. Yes, but do you hear it, smell it, taste it, feel it? Are you, too, caught up in that impetuous embrace? No? Ah, then your imagination is only half awake. No, it is not a question of background or actual experience now. There are enough familiar elements, as I have said before, to rouse your senses to vividly realize the picture as a whole if you will not shut the door to such realization--that door is your imagination. Open it! Open it! Now I shall close the book and ask the class to do likewise, while you read once more to us these first sentences, paint for us this picture. Yes, now you are using your imagination to stimulate my senses and awake my imagination, but you must take heed. You must let me enjoy this picture as a whole. You must let me see, feel, taste, smell, all "in the same breath." Remember it is a picture. Don't disregard its perspective. Let all the elements rest in proper relation one to another and to the whole--as George Eliot placed them when she made the setting. The atmosphere is on the whole full of peace. The river "hurries," but the "plain is wide"; the tide "rushes," but it is a "loving tide," even though its embrace be "impetuous." Try it once more! Is there not the joy of creation in such interpretation? Let us read on! You read to us still.

On this mighty tide the black ships--laden with the fresh-scented fir-planks, with rounded sacks of oil-bearing seed, or with dark glitter of coal--are borne along to the town of St. Ogg's, which shows its aged, fluted red roofs and the broad gables of its wharves between the low wooded hill and the river-brink, tingeing the water with a soft purple hue under the transient glance of this February sun. Far away on each hand stretch the rich pastures and the patches of dark earth, made ready for the seed of broad-leaved, green crops, or touched already with the tint of the tender-bladed autumn-sown corn. There is a remnant still of the last year's golden clusters of beehive ricks rising at intervals beyond the hedgerows; and everywhere the hedgerows are studded with trees: the distant ships seem to be lifting their masts and stretching their red-brown sails close among the branches of the spreading ash. Just by the red-roofed town the tributary Ripple flows with a lively current into the Floss. How lovely the little river is, with its dark, changing wavelets! It seems to me like a living companion while I wander along the bank and listen to its low, placid voice, as to the voice of one who is dear and loving. I remember these large, dipping willows. I remember the stone bridge.

And this is Dorlcote Mill. I must stand a minute or two here on the bridge and look at it, though the clouds are threatening, and it is far on in the afternoon. Even in this leafless time of departing February it is pleasant to look at--perhaps the chill, damp season adds a charm to the trimly kept, comfortable dwelling-house, as old as the elms and chestnuts that shelter it from the northern blast. The stream is brimful now, and lies high in this little withy plantation, and half drowns the grassy fringe of the croft in front of the house. As I look at the full stream, the vivid grass, the delicate bright-green powder softening the outline of the great trunks and branches that gleam from under the bare purple boughs, I am in love with moistness, and envy the white ducks that are dipping their heads far into the water here among the withes, unmindful of the awkward appearance they make in the drier world above.

The rush of the water and the booming of the mill bring a dreamy deafness, which seems to heighten the peacefulness of the scene. They are like a grand curtain of sound, shutting one out from the world beyond. And now there is the thunder of the huge covered wagon coming home with sacks of grain. That honest wagoner is thinking of his dinner, getting sadly dry in the oven at this late hour; but he will not touch it till he has fed his horses--the strong, submissive, meek-eyed beasts, who, I fancy, are looking mild reproach at him from between their blinkers, that he should crack his whip at them in that awful manner, as if they needed that hint! See how they stretch their shoulders up the slope toward the bridge, with all the more energy because they are so near home! Look at their grand shaggy feet, that seem to grasp the firm earth, at the patient strength of their neck, bowed under the heavy collar, at the mighty muscles of their struggling haunches! I should like well to hear them neigh over their hardly earned feed of corn, and see them, with their moist necks freed from the harness, dipping their eager nostrils into the muddy pond. Now they are on the bridge, and down they go again at a swifter pace, and the arch of the covered wagon disappears at the turning behind the trees.

Now I can turn my eyes toward the mill again, and watch the unresting wheel sending out its diamond jets of water. That little girl is watching it too: she has been standing on just the same spot at the edge of the water ever since I paused on the bridge. And that queer white cur with the brown ear seems to be leaping and barking in ineffectual remonstrance with the wheel; perhaps he is jealous, because his playfellow in the beaver bonnet is so rapt in its movement. It is time the little playfellow went in, I think; and there is a very bright fire to tempt her: the red light shines out under the deepening gray of the sky. It is time, too, for me to leave off resting my arms on the cold stone of this bridge.

Ah, my arms are really benumbed. I have been pressing my elbows on the arms of my chair and dreaming that I was standing on the bridge in front of Dorlcote Mill, as it looked one February afternoon many years ago. Before I dozed off, I was going to tell you what Mr. and Mrs. Tulliver were talking about as they sat by the bright fire in the left-hand parlor on that very afternoon I have been dreaming of.

If, in your interpretation of this passage, a sensitive imagination free, but controlled by vital thought and intelligent feeling, has found in trained instruments a lucid channel for expression, then, at the close of your reading, we, your auditors, shall find our arms really benumbed from pressing our elbows on the arms of our chairs as we dream with you that we are standing on the bridge in front of Dorlcote Mill--the Mill on the Floss, which we find on awakening is but the title and setting of a great author's great story.

We turn now to the second element of Narration--the characters. The setting we have just analyzed has introduced us to the main characters of a great story. Our interest is already awake to the little girl who has been watching with us the unresting wheel of the mill. Why not take Maggie Tulliver for our character study? To follow Maggie but a little way is to find Tom. This is well for us, because we need to study both types. Let us read from the chapter called "Tom Comes Home" in the life of the boy and girl.

TOM COMES HOME

Tom was to arrive early in the afternoon, and there was another fluttering heart besides Maggie's when it was late enough for the sound of the gig-wheels to be expected; for if Mrs. Tulliver had a strong feeling, it was fondness for her boy. At last the sound came--that quick light bowling of the gig-wheels--and in spite of the wind, which was blowing the clouds about, and was not likely to respect Mrs. Tulliver's curls and cap-strings, she came outside the door, and even held her hand on Maggie's offending head, forgetting all the griefs of the morning.

"There he is, my sweet lad! But Lord ha' mercy! he's got never a collar on; it's been lost on the road, I'll be bound, and spoiled the set."

Mrs. Tulliver stood with her arms open; Maggie jumped first on one leg and then on the other; while Tom descended from the gig, and said, with masculine reticence as to the tender emotions, "Hallo! Yap--what! are you there?"

Nevertheless, he submitted to be kissed willingly enough, though Maggie hung on his neck in rather a strangling fashion, while his blue-gray eyes wandered toward the croft and the lambs and the river, where he promised himself that he would begin to fish the first thing to-morrow morning. He was one of those lads that grow everywhere in England and at twelve or thirteen years of age look as much alike as goslings--a lad with light-brown hair, cheeks of cream and roses, full lips, indeterminate nose and eyebrows--a physiognomy in which it seems impossible to discern anything but the generic character of boyhood; as different as possible from poor Maggie's phiz, which Nature seemed to have molded and colored with the most decided intention. But that same Nature has the deep cunning which hides itself under the appearance of openness, so that simple people think they can see through her quite well, and all the while she is secretly preparing a refutation of their confident prophecies. Under these average boyish physiognomies that she seems to turn off by the gross, she conceals some of her most rigid, inflexible purposes, some of her most unmodifiable characters; and the dark-eyed, demonstrative, rebellious girl may after all turn out to be a passive being compared with this pink-and-white bit of masculinity with the indeterminate features.

"Maggie," said Tom, confidentially, taking her into a corner as soon as his mother was gone out to examine his box, and the warm parlor had taken off the chill he had felt from the long drive, "you don't know what I've got in my pockets," nodding his head up and down as a means of rousing her sense of mystery.

"No," said Maggie. "How stodgy they look, Tom! Is it marls (marbles) or cobnuts?" Maggie's heart sank a little, because Tom always said it was "no good" playing with her at those games--she played so badly.

"Marls! no; I've swopped all my marls with the little fellows, and cobnuts are no fun, you silly, only when the nuts are green. But see here!" He drew something half out of his right-hand pocket.

"What is it?" said Maggie, in a whisper. "I can see nothing but a bit of yellow."

"Why, it's ... a ... new ... guess, Maggie."

"Oh, I can't guess, Tom," said Maggie, impatiently.

"Don't be a spitfire, else I won't tell you," said Tom, thrusting his hand back into his pocket and looking determined.

"No, Tom," said Maggie, imploringly, laying hold of the arm that was held stiffly in the pocket. "I'm not cross, Tom; it was only because I can't bear guessing. Please be good to me."

Tom's arm slowly relaxed, and he said, "Well, then, it's a new fish-line--two new uns--one for you, Maggie, all to yourself. I wouldn't go halves in the toffee and ginger-bread on purpose to save the money; Gibson and Spouncer fought with me because I wouldn't. And here's hooks--see here! I say, won't we go and fish to-morrow down by Round Pool? And you shall catch your own fish, Maggie, and put the worms on, and everything--won't it be fun?"

Maggie's answer was to throw her arms around Tom's neck and hug him, and hold her cheek against his without speaking, while he slowly unwound some line, saying, after a pause:

"Wasn't I a good brother, now, to buy you a line all to yourself? You know, I needn't have bought it if I hadn't liked."

"Yes, very, very good. I do love you, Tom."

Tom had put the line back in his pocket, and was looking at the hooks one by one, before he spoke again.

"And the fellows fought me because I wouldn't give in about the toffee."

"Oh, dear! I wish they wouldn't fight at your school, Tom. Didn't it hurt you?"

"Hurt me? no," said Tom, putting up the hooks again, taking out a large pocket-knife, and slowly opening the largest blade, which he looked at meditatively as he rubbed his finger along it. Then he added:

"I gave Spouncer a black eye, I know--that's what he got by wanting to leather me; I wasn't going to go halves because anybody leathered me."

"Oh, how brave you are, Tom! I think you're like Samson. If there came a lion roaring at me, I think you'd fight him--wouldn't you, Tom?"

"How can a lion come roaring at you, you silly thing? There's no lions only in the shows."

"No; but if we were in the lion countries--I mean, in Africa, where it's very hot--the lions eat people there. I can show it to you in the book where I read it."

"Well, I should get a gun and shoot him."

"But if you hadn't got a gun--we might have gone out, you know, not thinking, just as we go fishing; and then a great lion might run toward us roaring, and we couldn't get away from him. What should you do, Tom?"

Tom paused, and at last turned away contemptuously, saying: "But the lion isn't coming. What's the use of talking?"

"But I like to fancy how it would be," said Maggie, following him. "Just think what you would do, Tom?"

"Oh, don't bother, Maggie! you're such a silly--I shall go and see my rabbits."

Maggie's heart began to flutter with fear. She dared not tell the sad truth at once, but she walked after Tom in trembling silence as he went out, thinking how she could tell him the news so as to soften at once his sorrow and anger; for Maggie dreaded Tom's anger of all things--it was quite a different anger from her own.

"Tom," she said, timidly, when they were out-of-doors, "how much money did you give for your rabbits?"

"Two half-crowns and a sixpence," said Tom, promptly.

"I think I've got a great deal more than that in my steel purse up-stairs. I'll ask mother to give it you."

"What for?" said Tom. "I don't want your money, you silly thing. I've got a great deal more money than you, because I'm a boy. I always have half-sovereigns and sovereigns for my Christmas boxes, because I shall be a man, and you only have five-shilling pieces, because you're only a girl."

"Well, but, Tom--if mother would let me give you two half-crowns and a sixpence out of my purse to put into your pocket to spend, you know, and buy some more rabbits with it?"

"More rabbits? I don't want any more."

"Oh, but, Tom, they're all dead."

Tom stopped immediately in his walk and turned round toward Maggie. "You forgot to feed 'em, then, and Harry forgot?" he said, his color heightening for a moment, but soon subsiding. "I'll pitch into Harry--I'll have him turned away. And I don't love you, Maggie. You sha'n't go fishing with me to-morrow. I told you to go and see the rabbits every day." He walked on again.

"Yes. But I forgot--and I couldn't help it, indeed, Tom. I'm so very sorry," said Maggie, while the tears rushed fast.

"You're a naughty girl," said Tom, severely, "and I'm sorry I bought you the fish-line. I don't love you."

"Oh, Tom, it's very cruel," sobbed Maggie. "I'd forgive you if you forgot anything--I wouldn't mind what you did--I'd forgive you and love you."

"Yes, you're a silly; but I never do forget things--I don't."

"Oh, please forgive me, Tom; my heart will break," said Maggie, shaking with sobs, clinging to Tom's arm, and laying her wet cheek on his shoulder.

Tom shook her off, and stopped again, saying in a peremptory tone: "Now, Maggie, you just listen. Aren't I a good brother to you?"

"Ye-ye-es," sobbed Maggie, her chin rising and falling convulsively.

"Didn't I think about your fish-line all this quarter, and mean to buy it, and saved my money o' purpose, and wouldn't go halves in the toffee, and Spouncer fought me because I wouldn't?"

"Ye-ye-es ... and I ... lo-lo-love you so, Tom."

"But you're a naughty girl. Last holidays you licked the paint off my lozenge-box, and the holidays before that you let the boat drag my fish-line down when I set you to watch it, and you pushed your head through my kite, all for nothing."

"But I didn't mean," said Maggie; "I couldn't help it."

"Yes, you could," said Tom, "if you'd minded what you were doing. And you're a naughty girl, and you sha'n't go fishing with me to-morrow."

With this terrible conclusion, Tom ran away from Maggie toward the mill, meaning to greet Luke there, and complain to him of Harry.

Maggie stood motionless, except from her sobs, for a minute or two; then she turned round and ran into the house, and up to her attic, where she sat on the floor, and laid her head against the worm-eaten shelf, with a crushing sense of misery. Tom was come home, and she had thought how happy she should be--and now he was cruel to her. What use was anything, if Tom didn't love her? Oh, he was very cruel! Hadn't she wanted to give him the money, and said how very sorry she was? She knew she was naughty to her mother, but she had never been naughty to Tom--had never meant to be naughty to him.

"Oh, he is cruel!" Maggie sobbed aloud, finding a wretched pleasure in the hollow resonance that came through the long empty space of the attic. She never thought of beating or grinding her Fetish; she was too miserable to be angry.

These bitter sorrows of childhood! when sorrow is all new and strange, when hope has not yet got wings to fly beyond the days and weeks, and the space from summer to summer seems measureless.

This text furnishes an easier exercise in interpretation, does it not? It does not require a great stretch of imagination to slip back five, ten, a dozen years to play with these children. But I cannot let you play with them. We want to meet and know them. The task for your imagination is not so simple as you think. It is called upon to engage in character interpretation. You cannot be allowed to merely watch Maggie and Tom play, or even to play with them. You must use your imagination to get inside the minds, hearts, souls of this boy and girl and reveal them to us. You must relive this scene for us, becoming first Maggie and then Tom. This exercise of your imagination belongs in its final and complete stage to the next and last of our studies, and to work on the drama; so we shall not demand too much of you along this line here, and I shall confine my suggestive analysis of the text to the following questions:

Define the relation existing between this brother and sister indicated by this scene.

Is this scene typical of their relation?

Is it a relation likely to obtain throughout their lives? Why?

Define the dispositions of these two children by applying to each three adjectives.

Will Maggie or Tom make the sacrifices inevitable to such a relation?

Characterize as to inflection and tone-color Maggie's voice and Tom's. (If your use of this book has been intelligently directed you have already made a study of these two elements of a vocal vocabulary--inflection and tone-color.)

Answer these questions and re-read the scene.

SELECTIONS FOR INTERPRETATION

The following selections were chosen for this study with a double concern in the choice,--concern for the development of imaginative vigor in vocal interpretation; concern for the development of a sense of plot in narrative composition. The demand upon the interpreter of any of these poems, for sensitive progressive play of imagination, in carrying an auditor through a series of events up to a critical issue, cannot fail to develop, with imaginative vigor, a new sensitiveness of creative instinct to the third element in narrative,--action.

Your imagination given free play can no more carry the "good news" from Ghent to Aix on this wild ride, and in the feat fail to outgrow all its former dimensions, than could the heart of Roland's master remain untouched in actually performing the feat itself.

HOW THEY BROUGHT THE GOOD NEWS FROM GHENT TO AIX[9]

[9] The "Good News" is that of the "Pacification de Gant," concluded in 1576. It was a treaty of union between Holland, Zealand, and the southern Netherlands, against Spain, under tyrannical Philip II. The treaty was greeted rapturously by the frontier cities, because it was expected to free the Netherlands from Spanish power.

"There is," writes Mr. Browning, "no sort of historical foundation about 'Good News from Ghent.' I wrote it under the bulwark of a vessel off the African coast, after I had been at sea long enough to appreciate even the fancy of a gallop on the back of a certain good horse 'York,' then in my stable at home. It was written in pencil on the fly-leaf of Bartoli's Simboli, I remember."

While there is, then, no historical foundation for the "gallop," the verisimilitude of the situation is perfect. Aix might easily have resolved to set herself on fire at a given hour, rather than submit herself and her citizens piecemeal to the torch of the persecutor. The "horse without peer" might possibly have galloped the ninety-odd miles between Ghent and Aix, but the feat would be a marvelous one.

This poem and "Herv?Riel," with the accompanying notes, are reprinted from Select Poems of Robert Browning, edited by William Rolfe, A.M., and H 闹 oise E. Hersey, and published by Harper & Brothers.

I

I sprang to the stirrup, and Joris, and he; I galloped, Dirck galloped, we galloped all three; "Good speed!" cried the watch, as the gate-bolts undrew; "Speed!" echoed the wall to us galloping through; Behind shut the postern, the lights sank to rest, And into the midnight we galloped abreast.

II

Not a word to each other; we kept the great pace Neck by neck, stride by stride, never changing our place; I turned in my saddle and made its girths tight, Then shortened each stirrup, and set the pique right, Rebuckled the check-strap, chained slacker the bit, Nor galloped less steadily Roland a whit.

III

'Twas moonset at starting; but while we drew near Lokeren, the cocks crew and twilight dawned clear; At Boom, a great yellow star came out to see; At Duffeld, 'twas morning as plain as could be; And from Mecheln church-steeple we heard the half chime, So Joris broke silence with, "Yet there is time!"

IV

At Aerschot, up leaped of a sudden the sun, And against him the cattle stood black every one, To stare through the mist at us galloping past; And I saw my stout galloper Roland at last, With resolute shoulders, each butting away The haze, as some bluff river headland its spray;

V

And his low head and crest, just one sharp ear bent back For my voice, and the other pricked out on his track; And one eye's black intelligence,--ever that glance O'er its white edge at me, his own master, askance! And the thick heavy spume-flakes which aye and anon His fierce lips shook upwards in galloping on.

VI

By Hasselt, Dirck groaned; and cried Joris, "Stay spur! Your Roos galloped bravely, the fault's not in her, We'll remember at Aix"--for one heard the quick wheeze Of her chest, saw the stretched neck and staggering knees, And sunk tail, and horrible heave of the flank, As down on her haunches she shuddered and sank.

VII

So we were left galloping, Joris and I, Past Looz and past Tongres, no cloud in the sky; The broad sun above laughed a pitiless laugh, 'Neath our feet broke the brittle bright stubble like chaff; Till over by Dalhem a dome-spire sprang white, And "Gallop," gasped Joris, "for Aix is in sight!

VIII

How they'll greet us!"--and all in a moment his roan Rolled neck and croup over, lay dead as a stone; And there was my Roland to bear the whole weight Of the news which alone could save Aix from her fate, With his nostrils like pits full of blood to the brim, And with circles of red for his eye-sockets' rim.

IX

Then I cast loose my buff-coat, each holster let fall, Shook off both my jack-boots, let go belt and all, Stood up in the stirrup, leaned, patted his ear, Called my Roland his pet-name, my horse without peer; Clapped my hands, laughed and sang, any noise, bad or good, Till at length into Aix Roland galloped and stood.

X

And all I remember is, friends flocking round As I sat with his head 'twixt my knees on the ground; And no voice but was praising this Roland of mine, As I poured down his throat our last measure of wine, Which (the burgesses voted by common consent) Was no more than his due who brought good news from Ghent.

--BROWNING.

LOCHINVAR

Oh, young Lochinvar is come out of the west, Through all the wide border his steed was the best; And save his good broadsword he weapon had none, He rode all unarmed, and he rode all alone. So faithful in love, and so dauntless in war, There never was knight like the young Lochinvar.

He stayed not for brake and he stopped not for stone, He swam the Esk river where ford there was none; But, ere he alighted at Netherby gate, The bride had consented, the gallant came late: For a laggard in love and a dastard in war Was to wed the fair Ellen of brave Lochinvar.

So boldly he entered the Netherby Hall, 'Mong bride's-men, and kinsmen, and brothers, and all; Then spoke the bride's father, his hand on his sword, For the poor craven bridegroom said never a word,-- "Oh, come ye in peace here, or come ye in war, Or to dance at our bridal, young Lord Lochinvar?"

"I long woo'd your daughter, my suit you denied; Love swells like the Solway, but ebbs like its tide; And now am I come, with this lost love of mine, To lead but one measure, drink one cup of wine. There are maidens in Scotland more lovely by far That would gladly be bride to the young Lochinvar."

The bride kissed the goblet, the knight took it up; He quaffed off the wine, and he threw down the cup; She looked down to blush, and she looked up to sigh, With a smile on her lip, and a tear in her eye. He took her soft hand, ere her mother could bar,-- "Now tread we a measure!" said young Lochinvar.

So stately his form, and so lovely her face, That never a hall such a galliard did grace; While her mother did fret, and her father did fume, And the bridegroom stood dangling his bonnet and plume, And the bride-maidens whispered, "'Twere better by far To have matched our fair cousin with young Lochinvar!"

One touch to her hand, and one word in her ear, When they reached the hall door, where the charger stood near; So light to the croup the fair lady he swung, So light to the saddle before her he sprung! "She is won! we are gone, over bank, bush, and scaur; They'll have fleet steeds that follow!" quoth young Lochinvar.

There was mounting 'mong Graemes of the Netherby clan:-- Fosters, Fenwicks, and Musgraves, they rode and they ran; There was racing and chasing on Cannobie Lea,-- But the lost bride of Netherby ne'er did they see. So daring in love, and so dauntless in war, Have ye e'er heard of gallant like young Lochinvar?

--WALTER SCOTT.

KING VOLMER AND ELSIE

After the Danish of Christian Winter

Where, over heathen doom-rings and gray stones of the Horg, In its little Christian city stands the church of Vordingborg, In merry mood King Volmer sat, forgetful of his power, As idle as the Goose of Gold that brooded on his tower.

Out spake the king to Henrik, his young and faithful squire: "Dar'st trust thy little Elsie, the maid of thy desire?" "Of all the men in Denmark she loveth only me: As true to me is Elsie as thy Lily is to thee."

Loud laughed the king: "To-morrow shall bring another day, When I myself will test her; she will not say me nay." Thereat the lords and gallants, that round about him stood, Wagged all their heads in concert and smiled as courtiers should.

The gray lark sings o'er Vordingborg, and on the ancient town From the tall tower of Valdemar the Golden Goose looks down: The yellow grain is waving in the pleasant wind of morn, The wood resounds with cry of hounds and blare of hunter's horn.

In the garden of her father little Elsie sits and spins, And, singing with the early birds, her daily task begins. Gay tulips bloom and sweet mint curls around her garden-bower, But she is sweeter than the mint and fairer than the flower.

About her form her kirtle blue clings lovingly, and, white As snow, her loose sleeves only leave her small, round wrists in sight; Below the modest petticoat can only half conceal The motion of the lightest foot that ever turned a wheel.

The cat sits purring at her side, bees hum in sunshine warm; But, look! she starts, she lifts her face, she shades it with her arm. And, hark! a train of horsemen, with sound of dog and horn, Come leaping o'er the ditches, come trampling down the corn!

Merrily rang the bridle-reins, and scarf and plume streamed gay, As fast beside her father's gate the riders held their way; And one was brave in scarlet cloak, with golden spur on heel, And, as he checked his foaming steed, the maiden checked her wheel.

"All hail among thy roses, the fairest rose to me! For weary months in secret my heart has longed for thee!" What noble knight was this? What words for modest maiden's ear? She dropped a lowly courtesy of bashfulness and fear.

She lifted up her spinning-wheel; she fain would seek the door, Trembling in every limb, her cheek with blushes crimsoned o'er. "Nay, fear me not," the rider said, "I offer heart and hand, Bear witness these good Danish knights who round about me stand.

I grant you time to think of this, to answer as you may, For to-morrow, little Elsie, shall bring another day." He spake the old phrase slyly as, glancing round his train, He saw his merry followers seek to hide their smiles in vain.

"The snow of pearls I'll scatter in your curls of golden hair, I'll line with furs the velvet of the kirtle that you wear; All precious gems shall twine your neck; and in a chariot gay You shall ride, my little Elsie, behind four steeds of gray.

And harps shall sound, and flutes shall play, and brazen lamps shall glow; On marble floors your feet shall weave the dances to and fro; At frosty eventide for us the blazing hearth shall shine, While, at our ease, we play at draughts, and drink the blood-red wine."

Then Elsie raised her head and met her wooer face to face; A roguish smile shone in her eye and on her lip found place. Back from her low white forehead the curls of gold she threw, And lifted up her eyes to his, steady and clear and blue.

"I am a lowly peasant, and you a gallant knight; I will not trust a love that soon may cool and turn to slight. If you would wed me henceforth be a peasant, not a lord; I bid you hang upon the wall your tried and trusty sword."

"To please you, Elsie, I will lay keen Dynadel away, And in its place will swing the scythe and mow your father's hay." "Nay, but your gallant scarlet cloak my eyes can never bear; A Vadmal coat, so plain and gray, is all that you must wear."

"Well, Vadmal will I wear for you," the rider gaily spoke, "And on the Lord's high altar I'll lay my scarlet cloak." "But mark," she said, "no stately horse my peasant love must ride, A yoke of steers before the plow is all that he must guide."

The knight looked down upon his steed: "Well, let him wander free,-- No other man must ride the horse that has been backed by me. Henceforth I'll tread the furrow and to my oxen talk, If only little Elsie beside my plow will walk."

"You must take from out your cellar cask of wine and flask and can; The homely mead I brew you may serve a peasant-man." "Most willingly, fair Elsie, I'll drink that mead of thine, And leave my minstrel's thirsty throat to drain my generous wine."

"Now break your shield asunder, and shatter sign and boss, Unmeet for peasant-wedded arms, your knightly knee across. And pull me down your castle from top to basement wall, And let your plow trace furrows in the ruins of your hall!"

Then smiled he with a lofty pride: right well at last he knew The maiden of the spinning-wheel was to her troth-plight true. "Ah, roguish little Elsie! you act your part full well: You know that I must bear my shield and in my castle dwell!

The lions ramping on that shield between the hearts aflame Keep watch o'er Denmark's honor, and guard her ancient name. For know that I am Volmer; I dwell in yonder towers, Who plows them plows up Denmark, this goodly home of ours!

I tempt no more, fair Elsie! your heart I know is true; Would God that all our maidens were good and pure as you! Well have you pleased your monarch, and he shall well repay: God's peace! Farewell! To-morrow will bring another day!"

He lifted up his bridle hand, he spurred his good steed then, And like a whirl-blast swept away with all his gallant men. The steel hoofs beat the rocky path; again on winds of morn The wood resounds with cry of hounds and blare of hunter's horn.

"Thou true and ever faithful!" the listening Henrik cried: And, leaping o'er the green hedge, he stood by Elsie's side. None saw the fond embracing, save, shining from afar, The Golden Goose that watched them from the tower of Valdemar.

O darling girls of Denmark! of all the flowers that throng Her vales of spring the fairest, I sing for you my song. No praise as yours so bravely rewards the singer's skill; Thank God! of maids like Elsie the land has plenty still!

--WHITTIER.

HERV?RIEL[10]

[10] "This spirited poem was sent to the Cornhill, because Browning was asked for a subscription to the fund for sending food to Paris after the siege by the Germans in 1870-71. Though he condemned Louis Napoleon's war, he wished to help the French in their distress, and he sent to the fund the 100 pounds that Mr. George Smith gave him for 'Herv?Riel.' The subject of the poem and its generous treatment surely manifolded the good-will of the gift. An English poet restored to France its 'Forgotten Worthy.' An Englishman sang the praises of a French sailor's balking the English fleet. One of the nation whose boast it is that her heroes need no other motive for their noble deeds than 'England expects every man to do his duty' showed that in France, too--whose citizens were accused of seeking glory and vainglory as their dearest gain--was a man who could act out Nelson's words with no thought of Nelson's end--a 'peerage or Westminster Abbey'--but just do his duty because it lay before him, and put aside with a smile the reward offered him for doing it; a real man, an honor to the nation and the navy of which he was part."

"The facts of the story had been forgotten and were denied at St. Malo, but the reports to the French Admiralty at the time were looked up and the facts established. Browning's only alteration is that Herv?Riel's holiday to see his wife, 'La Belle Aurore,' was to last, not a day only, but his lifetime."

"Herv?Riel" was written at Le Croisic, the home of the hero. It is a small fishing village near the mouth of the Loire.

I

On the sea and at the Hogue, sixteen hundred ninety-two, Did the English fight the French--woe to France! And, the thirty-first of May, helter-skelter thro' the blue, Like a crowd of frightened porpoises a shoal of sharks pursue,

Came crowding ship on ship to St. Malo on the Rance, With the English fleet in view.

II

'Twas the squadron that escaped, with the victor in full chase; First and foremost of the drove, in his great ship, Damfreville: Close on him fled, great and small, Twenty-two good ships in all; And they signaled to the place, 'Help the winners of a race! Get us guidance, give us harbor, take us quick--or, quicker still, Here's the English can and will!'

III

Then the pilots of the place put out brisk and leapt on board; 'Why, what hope or chance have ships like these to pass?' laughed they: 'Rocks to starboard, rocks to port, all the passage scarred and scored, Shall the Formidable here with her twelve and eighty guns Think to make the river-mouth by the single narrow way, Trust to enter where 'tis ticklish for a craft of twenty tons, And with flow at full beside? Now, 'tis slackest ebb of tide. Reach the mooring? Rather say, While rock stands or water runs, Not a ship will leave the bay!

IV

Then was called a council straight. Brief and bitter the debate: 'Here's the English at our heels; would you have them take in tow All that's left us of the fleet, linked together stern and bow, For a prize to Plymouth Sound? Better run the ships aground!' (Ended Damfreville his speech). Not a minute more to wait! 'Let the captains all and each Shove ashore, then blow up, burn the vessels on the beach! France must undergo her fate.

V

Give the word!' But no such word Was ever spoke or heard; For up stood, for out stepped, for in struck amid all these-- A captain? A lieutenant? A mate--first, second, third? No such man of mark, and meet With his betters to compete! But a simple Breton sailor pressed by Tourville for the fleet, A poor coasting-pilot he, Herv?Riel the Croisickese.

VI

And, 'What mockery or malice have we here?' cries Herv?Riel: 'Are you mad, you Malouins? Are you cowards, fools, or rogues? Talk to me of rocks and shoals, me who took the soundings, tell On my fingers every bank, every shallow, every swell 'Twixt the offing here and Grace, where the river disembogues? Are you bought by English gold? Is it love the lying's for? Morn and eve, night and day, Have I piloted your bay, Entered free and anchored fast at the foot of Solidor. Burn the fleet and ruin France? That were worse than fifty Hogues! Sirs, they know I speak the truth! Sirs, believe me there's a way! Only let me lead the line, Have the biggest ship to steer, Get this Formidable clear, Make the others follow mine, And I lead them, most and least, by a passage I know well, Right to Solidor past Grace, And there lay them safe and sound; And if one ship misbehave, Keel so much as grate the ground, Why, I've nothing but my life--here's my head!' cries Herv?Riel.

VII

Not a minute more to wait. 'Steer us in, then, small and great! Take the helm, lead the line, save the squadron!' cried its chief. Captains, give the sailor place! He is Admiral in brief. Still the north wind, by God's grace! See the noble fellow's face As the big ship, with a bound, Clears the entry like a hound, Keeps the passage as its inch of way were the wide sea's profound! See, safe thro' shoal and rock, How they follow in a flock, Not a ship that misbehaves, not a keel that grates the ground, Not a spar that comes to grief! The peril, see, is past, All are harbored, to the last, And just as Herv?Riel hollas 'Anchor!'--sure as fate Up the English come, too late!

VIII

So, the storm subsides to calm: They see the green trees wave On the heights o'erlooking Gr鑽e. Hearts that bled are stanched with balm, 'Just our rapture to enhance, Let the English rake the bay, Gnash their teeth and glare askance As they cannonade away! 'Neath rampired Solidor pleasant riding on the Rance!' How hope succeeds despair on each captain's countenance! Out burst all with one accord, 'This is Paradise for Hell! Let France, let France's King, Thank the man that did the thing!' What a shout, and all one word, 'Herv?Riel!' As he stepped in front once more, Not a symptom of surprise In the frank blue Breton eyes, Just the same man as before.

IX

Then said Damfreville, 'My friend, I must speak out at the end, Though I find the speaking hard. Praise is deeper than the lips; You have saved the King his ships, You must name your own reward. Faith our sun was near eclipse! Demand whate'er you will, France remains your debtor still. Ask to heart's content and have! or my name's not Damfreville.'

X

Then a beam of fun outbroke On the bearded mouth that spoke, As the honest heart laughed through Those frank eyes of Breton blue: 'Since I needs must say my say, Since on board the duty's done, And from Malo Roads to Croisic Point, what is it but a run?-- Since 'tis ask and have, I may-- Since the others go ashore-- Come! A good whole holiday! Leave to go, and see my wife, whom I call the Belle Aurore!' That he asked and that he got--nothing more.

XI

Name and deed alike are lost: Not a pillar nor a post In his Croisic keeps alive the feat as it befell; Not a head in white and black On a single fishing smack, In memory of the man but for whom had gone to wrack All that France saved from the fight whence England bore the bell. Go to Paris: rank on rank Search the heroes flung pell-mell On the Louvre, face and flank! You shall look long enough ere you come to Herv?Riel. So, for better and for worse, Herv?Riel, accept my verse! In my verse, Herv?Riel, do thou once more Save the squadron, honor France, love thy wife the Bell Aurore!

Your imagination can no more follow the flight of the Formidable, steered by Herv?Riel, with the French fleet close following her guidance and "the English at her heels" past the rocks and shoals of Grace to safe harbor at Solidor, and remain creatively unsensitive to the pulse of progressive action, than could the actual rescue of his country's squadron leave unmoved toward the "man who did the deed" the heart of her Captain Damfreville.

And when your imagination has not only carried you through such adventure, but stimulated my imagination to like activity, there is no limit to be set to the development which may result for us both.

Suggestive analysis can be of little help at this point, the work must be done in the class-room under direction.

To such stimulating exercise in the vocal interpretation of these poems of action, I leave you and your imagination. I shall hope to find difficulty in recognizing either of you at our next meeting. Like Mr. Rhoades's[11] pupil when he emerged from the Ninth book of Paradise Lost, you ought to have "outgrown all your present intellectual clothes" in the study of these stories in verse.

[11] Read The Training of the Imagination, by James Rhoades; John Lane Publishing Company.

As further material for this study there is no better choice to be made than Tennyson's great quasi-epic, The Idylls of the King, from which but for lack of space we should have printed selections. The following suggestions for work in composition at this point are based on the Idylls.

Describe in your own words Camelot.

Write an imaginary scene between Gareth and his mother.

Tell the story of Elaine.

Make the Holy Grail into the form of a miracle play.

FIFTH STUDY

TO DEVELOP DRAMATIC INSTINCT

Our final study in interpretation has for its concern the development of dramatic instinct. The work just finished should have left no doubt in your mind as to the nature or value of this final step in the training, since it has anticipated both. Development of imaginative vigor should arouse a latent dramatic instinct and release histrionic power. The choice of place in these studies for this phase of the training was made to insure cumulative evolution resulting in balanced expression. As imagination needs to safeguard her freedom with sympathetic thought and intelligent emotion, so dramatic instinct needs the guidance of a vigorous but trained imagination. Dramatic instinct so directed should achieve skill in interpreting drama and lead to distinction in the art of acting. The immediate evolution should be a clarified vision of life. Your final attainment from this theory should be distinction in the art of living.

With dramatic instinct capable of such achievement, let us proceed to exercise it in the material chosen for this study,--dramatic literature. The natural transition from story to play, from narrative to drama, is by way of the monologue. Some discussion with suggestive analysis of this form is necessary in order to impress upon you the difference between suggestive impersonation and actual impersonation or characterization, leading to a clear understanding of the difference between reading a play and acting in one; but the final evolution of interpretative power must come through acted drama,--through taking part in a play.

The dictionary in defining the monologue authorizes three forms: (1) when the actor tells a continuous story in which he is the chief character, referring to the others as absent; (2) when he assumes the voice or manner of several characters successively; (3) more recently, when he implies that the others are present, leading the audience to imagine what they say by his replies. Browning created this more recent form, which is the most vital of the three. I have chosen for your study of the monologue examples from Browning alone. To interpret effectively any one of the Browning monologues will call into play every element of power in voice and expression which you have gained in your study of previous forms. You must think vividly, feel intelligently, realize and suggest an atmosphere, sustain a situation, and keep the beauty of the poetic form. And you must do all this in the person of another. The new demand which the monologue makes is impersonation. Let us see just what we mean by impersonation. It is the art of identifying one's self with the character to be portrayed. It is the art of losing one's self in the character and the situation the dramatist has created. This means that the spirit of the character must take possession of the impersonator, and inform his every thought and feeling, and so his every motion and tone. Remember, it is the spirit of the character that must determine the nature of the tone and gesture. The great danger in entering upon the study of impersonation lies in emphasizing the outward manifestation instead of the inward spirit of the character to be portrayed. If you really sense the soul, mind, heart quality of the character you are to present, and have made your voice and body free agents for the manifestation of those qualities, your impersonation will be convincing. If the spirit of the Patriot or Andrea del Sarto or Fra Lippo Lippi or Pompilia or Caponsacchi or Guido obsesses you, the outward manifestation will take care of itself--always provided your instruments are responsive. Don't begin with the outward manifestation. Don't say I think this man would frown a great deal, or fold his arms over his breast, or use an eyeglass, or strut, or stoop, or do any one of a hundred things which, if repeated a half-dozen times during an impersonation, may become a mannerism and get between the audience and the spirit of the character. When you are studying a character for the purpose of impersonation determine first to what type it belongs. Then study that type, wherever you are. Daily life becomes your teacher and studio. When you enter upon this art there are no longer dull moments in railroad stations or trains, in shops or in the social whirl. Everywhere and always you are the student seeking to know and understand types of people better, that you may use your knowledge in presenting to an audience an individual. When you have caught the spirit of the individual you must realize the situation out of which this particular individual speaks.

Let us make a special study of the Tale (Browning's epilogue to The Two Poets of Croisic). It is perhaps the most exquisite of the poet's creations in this field. The situation reveals a young girl recalling to her poet lover an old Greek tale he had once told her. There is a suggestion from some critics that Browning has drawn his wife in this portrait, and through it pays his tribute to her. This immediately affords us a clue to the type of character to which the speaker belongs. We cannot hope (nor do we wish) to impersonate Mrs. Browning, but a knowledge of Mrs. Browning and her relation to her poet lover, gained through a study of her Letters and Sonnets, will lead us more quickly to a comprehension of the speaker and situation in the Tale.

Obsessed by the spirit of the character and fully realizing the situation, our next step is, in imagination, to set the stage. This is an important point in presenting a monologue. The impersonator must have a clear idea of his position on his imaginary stage relative to his imaginary interlocutor. But he must remember that imaginary stage-setting admits of only delicately suggestive use. This is true of the handling of a monologue at every point. It must be suggestive. The actor carries to completion the action which the monologuist suggests. The art of interpreting a monologue depends upon the discrimination of the impersonator in drawing his line between suggestion and actualization in gesture. The business of the monologuist is to make an appeal to the imagination of the audience so vivid that the imagination of the audience can actualize the suggestion. And the illusion is complete. What are the relative positions of the girl and her lover in the Tale? There is nothing in the lines to make our choice arbitrary. It is only important that we determine a relation and keep it consistently throughout the reading. Here is a possible "setting." They are in the poet's study; he is working at his desk; she is sitting in a great chair before the fire, a book in her hand, which she does not read; she is gazing into the flames. She begins dreamily, more to herself than to him--"What a pretty tale you told me." At what point does her tone lose its reflective quality and become more personal? Where does she turn to him? How do we know that he leaves his chair and comes over to sit on the arm of her chair? What calls him to her? What two qualities of feeling run through her mood and determine the color of her tone and the character of her movements. If your study of Mrs. Browning has been intelligent, this interplay of the whimsical and serious in her nature cannot have escaped you, and it will illumine now your impersonation of this girl. It is the secret of the peculiar charm of this creation. The story she tells is an old and well-known one. It is the manner of the telling through which we come in touch with an exquisite woman's soul that holds us spellbound. Unless the interpreter catches this secret and reveals it to his audience, he will miss the distinctive feature of the monologue and reduce it to a narrative poem.

A TALE

I

What a pretty tale you told me Once upon a time --Said you found it somewhere (scold me!) Was it prose or was it rhyme, Greek or Latin? Greek, you said, While your shoulder propped my head.

II

Anyhow there's no forgetting This much if no more, That a poet (pray, no petting!) Yes, a bard, sir, famed of yore, Went where such like used to go, Singing for a prize, you know.

III

Well, he had to sing, nor merely Sing but play the lyre; Playing was important clearly Quite as singing: I desire, Sir, you keep the fact in mind For a purpose that's behind.

IV

There stood he, while deep attention Held the judges round, --Judges able, I should mention, To detect the slightest sound Sung or played amiss: such ears Had old judges, it appears!

V

None the less he sang out boldly, Played in time and tune, Till the judges, weighing coldly Each note's worth, seemed, late or soon, Sure to smile 'In vain one tries Picking faults out: take the prize!'

VI

When, a mischief! Were they seven Strings the lyre possessed? Oh, and afterward eleven, Thank you! Well, sir--who had guessed Such ill luck in store?--it happed One of those same seven strings snapped.

VII

All was lost, then! No! a cricket (What 'cicada'? Pooh!) --Some mad thing that left its thicket For mere love of music--flew With its little heart on fire, Lighted on the crippled lyre.

VIII

So that when (Ah, joy!) our singer For his truant string Feels with disconcerted finger, What does cricket else but fling Fiery heart forth, sound the note Wanted by the throbbing throat?

IX

Ay and, ever to the ending, Cricket chirps at need, Executes the hands intending, Promptly, perfectly,--indeed Saves the singer from defeat With her chirrup low and sweet.

X

Till, at ending, all the judges Cry with one assent 'Take the prize--a prize who grudges Such a voice and instrument? Why, we took your lyre for harp, So it shrilled us forth F sharp!'

XI

Did the conqueror spurn the creature, Once its service done? That's no such uncommon feature In the case when Music's son Finds his Lotte's power too spent For aiding soul-development.

XII

No! This other, on returning Homeward, prize in hand, Satisfied his bosom's yearning: (Sir, I hope you understand!) --Said 'Some record there must be Of this cricket's help to me!'

XIII

So, he made himself a statue: Marble stood, life-size; On the lyre, he pointed at you, Perched his partner in the prize; Never more apart you found Her, he throned, from him, she crowned.

XIV

That's the tale: its application? Somebody I know Hopes one day for reputation Thro' his poetry that's--oh, All so learned and so wise And deserving of a prize!

XV

If he gains one, will some ticket, When his statue's built, Tell the gazer "Twas a cricket Helped my crippled lyre, whose lilt Sweet and low, when strength usurped Softness' place i' the scale, she chirped?

XVI

For as victory was nighest, While I sang and played-- With my lyre at lowest, highest, Right alike,--one string that made "Love" sound soft was snapt in twain, Never to be heard again,--

XVII

Had not a kind cricket fluttered, Perched upon the place Vacant left, and duly uttered "Love, Love, Love," whene'er the bass Asked the treble to atone For its somewhat somber drone.'

XVIII

But you don't know music! Wherefore Keep on casting pearls To a--poet? All I care for Is--to tell him that a girl's 'Love' comes aptly in when gruff Grows his singing. (There, enough!)

INCIDENT OF THE FRENCH CAMP

I

You know, we French stormed Ratisbon: A mile or so away, On a little mound, Napoleon Stood on our storming-day; With neck out-thrust, you fancy how, Legs wide, arms locked behind, As if to balance the prone brow Oppressive with its mind.

II

Just as perhaps he mused 'My plans That soar, to earth may fall, Let once my army-leader Lannes Waver at yonder wall,'-- Out 'twixt the battery smokes there flew A rider, bound on bound Full-galloping; nor bridle drew Until he reached the mound.

III

Then off there flung in smiling joy, And held himself erect By just his horse's mane, a boy: You hardly could suspect-- (So tight he kept his lips compressed, Scarce any blood came through) You looked twice ere you saw his breast Was all but shot in two.

IV

'Well,' cried he, 'Emperor, by God's grace We've got you Ratisbon! The Marshal's in the market-place, And you'll be there anon To see your flag-bird flap his vans Where I, to heart's desire, Perched him!' The chief's eye flashed; his plans Soared up again like fire.

V

The chief's eye flashed; but presently Softened itself, as sheathes A film the mother-eagle's eye When her bruised eaglet breathes; 'You're wounded!' 'Nay,' the soldier's pride Touched to the quick, he said: 'I'm killed, Sire!' And his chief beside, Smiling the boy fell dead.

MY LAST DUCHESS

FERRARA

That's my last Duchess painted on the wall, Looking as if she were alive. I call That piece a wonder, now: Fr?Pandolf's hands Worked busily a day, and there she stands. Will 't please you sit and look at her? I said 'Fr?Pandolf' by design; for never read Strangers like you that pictured countenance, The depth and passion of its earnest glance, But to myself they turned (since none puts by The curtain I have drawn for you, but I) And seemed as they would ask me, if they durst, How such a glance came there; so, not the first Are you to turn and ask thus. Sir, t'was not Her husband's presence only, called that spot Of joy into the Duchess' cheek: perhaps Fr?Pandolf chanced to say 'Her mantle laps Over my lady's wrist too much,' or 'Paint Must never hope to reproduce the faint Half-flush that dies along her throat': such stuff Was courtesy, she thought, and cause enough For calling up that spot of joy. She had A heart--how shall I say?--too soon made glad, Too easily impressed; she liked whate'er She looked on, and her looks went everywhere. Sir, 'twas all one! My favor at her breast, The dropping of the daylight in the West, The bough of cherries some officious fool Broke in the orchard for her, the white mule She rode with round the terrace--all and each Would draw from her alike the approving speech, Or blush, at least. She thanked men,--good! but thanked Somehow--I know not how--as if she ranked My gift of a nine-hundred-years-old name With anybody's gift. Who'd stoop to blame This sort of trifling? Even had you skill In speech--(which I have not)--to make your will Quite clear to such an one, and say, 'Just this Or that in you disgusts me; here you miss, Or there exceed the mark'--and if she let Herself be lessoned so, nor plainly set Her wits to yours, forsooth, and made excuse, --E'en then would be some stooping; and I choose Never to stoop. Oh sir, she smiled, no doubt, Whene'er I passed her; but who passed without Much the same smile? This grew; I gave commands; Then all smiles stopped together. There she stands As if alive. Will 't please you rise? We'll meet The company below, then. I repeat, The Count your master's known munificence Is ample warrant that no just pretense Of mine for dowry will be disallowed; Though his fair daughter's self, as I avowed At starting, is my object. Nay, we'll go Together down, sir. Notice Neptune, though, Taming a sea-horse, thought a rarity, Which Claus of Innsbruck cast in bronze for me!

--BROWNING.

Our last form for interpretative vocal study is the play. We shall discover that the presentation of the play makes the same demands upon the interpreter as the monologue with the new element of transition. We are still studying the monologue, because we are to read, not act, the play. It is still suggestive, not actualized impersonation. But instead of one character to suggestively set forth we have two, three, a dozen to present. The transition from character to character becomes our one new problem. As we have said before, in making the transition from character to character, voice, mind, and body must be so volatile that the action of the play shall not be interrupted. I know of no better way to enter upon the study of a play for reading (or acting) than to treat each character as the speaker in a monologue of the Browning type. The danger in transition from character to character centers in the instant's pause when one speaker yields to another. The unskilful reader loses both characters at this point and becomes conscious of himself; the action of the play stops; and the illusion of scene and situation is lost. The great reader of the play (in that instant's pause), as he utters the last word of one character, becomes the interlocutor listening to the words which he as the other character has just uttered. In that instant he must show the effect of the speech he has just uttered upon the character he has just become. Which is the greater art: to read a play, or to act in it?

Use for your study of the play the Shakespearian drama. Begin with scenes from As You Like It and The Merchant of Venice; but begin with actualized impersonation of the characters. No discussion more! No analysis more! The play--the "play's the thing" through which to complete this evolution in Vocal Expression.

A FINAL WORD ON INTERPRETATION

Looking back over these studies in interpretation, let us review in true scholastic fashion the main points thus far discovered. We say looking back, but as far as the arrangement of our text goes this review involves looking forward too. The division of the book into three parts is purely a matter of a necessary separation in discussing the three activities involved in vocal expression. If your use of this book has been intelligent, each study in interpretation has revealed your need to strengthen your vocal vocabulary or to perfect your vocal technique, and you have turned at once for the required help to the studies in Part II and the exercises in Part III.

Omitting a review of the preliminary plunge, which was intended to "show up" all your peculiar powers and all your especial needs at once, and so furnish a basis for the main work, let us see what happened in the five following studies. It will simplify our statement in each case to base the analysis of our discoveries on the form of literature employed in each study.

You found then (or ought to have found) in Study One: that the essay and didactic poem make a fundamental appeal to the mind; that the demand upon the interpreter of this form is for clear, concise thinking; that your need is for a command of unerring emphasis and purposeful inflection. You turned to the studies in pause, change of pitch, and inflection to meet that need.

Returning to the main study, you tested your vocal skill on the essay to find the essay so read might persuade an auditor to some readjustment of his ideas, values, discriminations, or strengthen him in convictions already held.

Study Two revealed that in lyric poetry the primary appeal is to emotion; that its vocal demand upon the interpreter is for a mastery of tone-color, a sense of rhythm, and the power to suggest a background of musical sound. Having supplied as far as possible any lack in your vocabulary or technique by supplementary work in Parts II and III, returning you found that a lyric rightly read could release in the auditor pity, forgiveness, forbearance, endurance, understanding, love.

The Third Study should have convinced you that a sense of good humor is a safe and desirable thing to cultivate; that the whimsical tone in interpretation will leaven almost any lump of sheer learning and counteract a serious overdose of sentiment; that fable, fairy tale, and nonsense rhyme depend too for successful interpretation upon this element of whimsicality in the reader; that the secret of the whimsical element in vocal expression lies in a use of pause and inflection.

Study Four should have discovered to you that the three elements of the short story can only be realized through imagination; that imaginative vigor dealing with action requires sustained vitality of tone. Such discovery should have resulted in many hours of work on the exercises for support and freedom of tone.

When you reached the Fifth and last Study, the work in monologue and drama should have easily awakened your dramatic instinct and quickly released your histrionic power. You should have learned through monologue and drama to understand various types of persons; to see more clearly the relations of men and events; to more intelligently comprehend life itself.

Finally, we have discovered that to become a true interpreter of literature means to become a lucid channel for the message of an author to the mind of an auditor,--nay, that it means more than that. In final evolution the interpreter of literature becomes a revealer of life. The final effect of literature worth interpreting is to enlarge the world's knowledge of life's beauty, truth, or power. Your final concern as an interpreter is to let life find through you uninterrupted revelation on one of these planes; to become a pure medium between the beauty, truth, and power of life and the seeking soul. The author need not be considered in this final analysis, because you, the interpreter, first became identified with the author, and then both of you are lost in the vision, save only as either personality may enlarge or clarify the revelation.

A personal experience may help you to realize this ideal of the interpreter's art.

With a sense of protest, I had presented a play I loved to an audience with which I felt little sympathy. By chance there was in that audience one of our best teachers and critics. After my recital I sought his criticism. Beginning, as the true critic always should, with a noting of some point of power, he said, "I congratulate you upon your illumined moments, but--they are too infrequent. You must multiply them." "What do you mean by my illumined moments?" I asked. "The moments when you do not get between your audience and the thought you are uttering--the moments when you become a revealer of life to them. Your attitude toward your audience is not sustained in the simplicity and clearness of some of its moments. You suddenly ring down the curtain in the middle of the scene. That spoils the scene, you know. You seem to feel a revolt against the giving of your confidence to the audience, and thereupon you immediately shut them away. You become conscious of yourself, and we, the audience, lose the vision and become conscious of you and the way you are reading or reciting or acting." Then he added, "Adelaide Neilson, at first, had illumined moments in her playing of Juliet, but finally her impersonation became one piece of illumination." That delightful teacher, reader, and critic, the late Mr. Howard Ticknor, suggested the same ideal in comparing a Juliet of to-day with Miss Neilson's Juliet. "When Miss ---- is on the balcony," he said, "you hear all around you: 'How lovely she looks!' 'Isn't that robe dear?' 'How beautiful her voice is!' When Miss Neilson lived that little minute, a breathless people prayed with Juliet, 'I would not for the world they found thee here,' and sighed with Romeo--'O blessed, blessed night! I am afeard, being in night, all this is but a dream.'" Miss Neilson was Juliet. They, the audience, lived with these lovers one hour of lyric rapture, and could never again be quite so commonplace in their attitude toward the "deathless passion." They may not now remember Adelaide Neilson, but they remember that story, and forever carry a new vision of life and love, because the actress lost herself in the life of the play. She did not exploit her personality and let it stand between the audience and the drama. When some one says to you--the reader or actress, "I shall never forget the way you raised your eyebrow at that point," don't stop to reply, but fly to your study and read the lines "at that point" over and over, with level brows, until you understand the meaning, and can express the thought so effectively by a lift of your voice that you no longer need the help of your eyebrow. Every gesture, every tone, must call attention, not to itself, but to the hidden meaning of the author. It must illumine the text of the character portrayed. That is it: if we would be artists (and there is not one among us who would not be an artist) we must cease to put our little selves in front of our messages. In the home, in the office, in the houses of our friends, in the school-room, on the platform, on the stage, let us be simple, natural, sincere. Let us lay aside our mannerisms. Let us seek to know and reveal life. Then shall we be remembered--not, for a queer way of combing our hair, or lifting our eyes, or using our hands, or shrugging our shoulders, but for some revelation of truth or of beauty which we have brought to a community.

PART II

STUDIES IN VOCAL EXPRESSION

THE VOCAL VOCABULARY

There is a theory that it is dangerous to go beyond the mere freeing of the instrument in either vocal or physical training. In accordance with this theory I was advised by a well-known actress to confine my study for the stage, so far as the vocal and pantomimic preparation was concerned, to singing, dancing, and fencing. "Get your voice and body under control," she said. "Make them free, but don't connect shades of thought and emotion with definite tones of the voice or movements of the body; don't meddle with Delsarte or elocution." This advice seemed good at the time. It still seems to me that it ought to be the right method. But I have grown to distrust it. One of the chief sources of my distrust has been the effect of the theory upon the art of the actress who gave the advice. She is perhaps the most graceful woman on the stage to-day, and her voice is pure music. But her gestures and tones fail in lucidity; they fail to illumine the text of the part she essays to interpret. One grows suddenly impatient of the meaningless grace of her movements, the meaningless music of her voice. One longs for a swift--if studied--stride across the stage in anger instead of the unstudied grace of her glide in swirling-robed protest. One longs to hear a staccato declaration of intention instead of the cadenced music of a voice guiltless of intention. No! After the body has been made a free and responsive agent, a mastery of certain fundamental laws, a mastery of certain principles of gesture in accordance with the dictates of thought and emotion, is necessary to its further perfecting as a vivid, powerful, and true agent of personality. The action must be suited to the word, the word to the action, through a study of the laws governing expression in action.

So with the voice: to become not only a free instrument, but a beautiful and powerful means of expression and communication it must learn to recognize and obey certain fundamental laws governing its modulations. A master of verbal expression is distinguished by his vast vocabulary of words, and his skill and discrimination in its use. A master of vocal expression must acquire what we may call a vocal vocabulary, consisting of changes of pitch, varieties of inflection and variations in tone color, and must know how to use these elements with skill and discrimination. Our need for such a vocabulary was discovered to us at every step of the work in interpretation. The suggestions and exercises of the following studies aim to supplement the work in interpretation by meeting that need. Before making a detailed study of each element of this vocal vocabulary let us make a quick study with the four elements in mind. Remember, in the last preliminary exercise, as in the final complete interpretative endeavor, the material we employ is to be chosen from real literature. It is to be worth interpreting whether it be a single line or phrase or a complete poetical drama. We have agreed to consider literature as real literature, and so worth our interpretative efforts, when it possesses one or combines all of the three qualities,--beauty, truth, and power.

This passage from Emerson's Friendship surely meets that requirement. It is truth beautifully and powerfully expressed. It will serve.

Our friendships hurry to short and poor conclusions because we have made them a texture of wine and dreams instead of the tough fiber of the human heart.

Having read this passage cursorily (as is the custom in reading to one's self to-day), will you now study it for a moment very closely. Now, once more, please, read it silently, noting the action of your mind as you read. ("Watch its pulsations," Dr. Curry would say.) And now, aloud, although without an auditor, read it, this time noting the effect of the action of the mind upon your voice. Did its pitch change? Where and why? How did you inflect the words "wine and dreams"? How did the inflection of these words differ from that of the last six words, "tough fiber of the human heart," with which they are contrasted in thought? Did your tone change color at any point? Why? Where? But now, once more, let us approach the passage, this time with a different intention. Let us study it with the idea of interpreting it for another mind. Now the method of attack is very different. Not that it ought to be different. But it is. Intense concentration ought to characterize all our reading, whether its object be to acquire knowledge or pleasure for one's self, or to impart either to another. But the day of reading which "maketh a full man" seems to be long past, so far as the general public is concerned. The necessity of skimming the pages of a dozen fourth-rate books of the hour in order to be at least a lucid interlocutor, and so a desired dinner guest, is making our reading a swift gathering of colorless impressions which may remain a week or only a day, and which leave no lasting effect of beauty or truth upon the mind and heart of the reader. Should it not be rather an intense application of the mind to the thought of a master mind, until that thought, in all its power and beauty, has broadened the boundaries of the reader's mind and enlarged the meaning of all his thoughts? I wonder if a much smaller proportion of time spent in such reading might not result in a less bromidic social atmosphere, even though its tendency were a bit serious. I think it might be both safe and interesting to try such an experiment.

But now we must return to Emerson on Friendship. In studying a passage for the purpose of vocal interpretation you have learned that the concentration of attention upon the thought must be intense, you must make the thought absolutely your own before you can present it to your auditor, it must possess you before you can express it; that the thought must seem in the moment of its expression to be a creation of your own brain, it must belong to you as only the thing you have created can, and until you have so recreated the thought it is not yours to give. Having recalled these precepts, read the passage silently again. Pour upon it the light of your experience, your philosophy, your ideals, your perception of truth. Comment upon it silently as you read. Now read it aloud and let your voice do this commenting.

But wait a moment. Let me quote for you the paragraph following this statement.

The laws of friendship are austere and eternal, of one web with the laws of nature and morals. But we have aimed at a swift and petty benefit to suck a sudden sweetness. We snatch at the slowest fruit in the whole garden of God, which many summers and many winters must ripen.

This is Emerson's paraphrase of his original statement. How much of it did your mental commentary include? How did your silent paraphrase resemble this? Read the original passage again to yourself in the light of this paraphrase. I shall ask you now to repeat the first sentence from memory, for you will find, after this concentrated contemplation of a thought, that its form is fixed fast in your mind. That is a delightful accompaniment of this kind of reading. The form of the thought, if it be apposite (which it must be to be literature, and we are considering only literature), the form of a thought so approached stays with us in all its beauty.

Let us then repeat the original statement, having read the passage in which Emerson has elaborated it. Now, what you must demand of your voice is this: that it shall so handle the single introductory sentence as to suggest the rest of the paragraph. In other words, your voice must do the paraphrasing, by means of its changes in pitch, its inflections, and its variations in tone-color; by means, in short, of its vocal vocabulary.

I

STUDY IN PAUSE AND CHANGE OF PITCH

It is asserted that, "the last word has not been said on any subject." Mr. Hamilton Mabie seemed to me to achieve a last word on the subject of pause when he casually remarked: "Emerson was a master of pause; he would pause, and into the pool of expectancy created by that pause drop just the right word." There seems little to be added to complete the exposition of that single sentence. It surely leaves no doubt in our minds as to the effect to be desired from the use of this element of our vocabulary. How to use it to gain that effect is our problem. First of all, we must cease to be afraid to pause. We hurry on over splendid opportunities to elucidate our text through a just use of this form of emphasis, beset by two fears: fear that we shall seem to have forgotten the text; fear that we shall actually forget it if we stop to think. Think of being afraid to stop to think lest we should stop thinking! That is precisely what the fear indicates. It arises, of course, from a confusion as to the real nature of pause. We confuse pause with its ghost, hesitation. Dr. Curry makes the difference clear for us in his definition of hesitation as an "empty pause." "Empty of what?" you ask. Empty of thought! Of course, an empty pause is a ghastly as well as a ghostly thing to experience. If you have ever faced an audience in one of those "awful" moments when your voice has ceased because your thought has stopped, and when you are painfully aware of a pool of embarrassed sympathy into which you know there is no word to drop, then you have learned the meaning of an empty pause.

On the other hand, if you shall ever face an audience in one of those fateful moments when your voice pauses because your thought is so vital, that you realize both your audience and you must be given time to fully grasp it, and when you are serenely conscious of that "pool of expectancy" into which you know you have just the right word to drop, then you will learn the meaning of a true pause.

Some one has called inflection a running commentary of the emotions upon the thought. Emphasis might well be defined in the same way. The definition would need to be a bit more inclusive, since emphasis includes inflection. Emphasis then may be defined as a running commentary of the thought and emotion of the reader upon the thought of the text he interprets. The words reveal the thought; your valuation of that thought, as you interpret it, is revealed through your vocal vocabulary in voicing it. We, your auditors, can only gather from your emphasis your valuation of the truth or importance of what you are uttering. You may use one or all of the elements of your vocal vocabulary to bring out the thought of a single phrase. The elements of the vocal vocabulary are all forms of emphasis.

Since pause is a cessation of speech it can hardly be called an element of a vocal vocabulary; but it may rightly be called the basis of our vocabulary because it determines our use of the other elements. It behooves us then to make a study of pause before testing our vocabulary as to its other elements.

Here are two texts to be valued by our use of the pause.

EXTRACT FROM THE DIARY OF A BOARDING-SCHOOL GIRL

At midnight, the magic hour as every girl knows for affairs of a purely private and personal nature, when far away at the end of a corridor you can almost hear Miss ----'s peaceful snore, when as the poet aptly put it in this morning's English stunt, "darkness clears our vision which by day is sun-blind"--(I thought Jane and I would die laughing and give it all away when we came to that line in Mr. Lanier's stupid poem),--well, as I say, exactly at that hour my heart began to beat so hard I thought it would wake Madge without the "punch" I had promised to give her when it was time to begin preparations for our grand spread.

From Sidney Lanier's Crystal.

At midnight, death's and truth's unlocking time. When far within the spirit's hearing rolls The great soft rumble of the course of things-- A bulk of silence in a mask of sound,-- When darkness clears our vision that by day Is sun-blind, and the soul's a ravening owl For truth and flitteth here and there about Low-lying woody tracts of time and oft Is minded for to sit upon a bough, Dry-dead and sharp, of some long-stricken tree And muse in that gaunt place,--'twas then my heart, Deep in the meditative dark, cried out: ...

The same hour, midnight, is designated by both girl and poet; the same two words, "at midnight," open the confession and the poem. A pause must follow these words in the reading of either text, and another pause must be made after the qualifying phrase which immediately follows the opening words of either text. But what a difference in the comparative length of the pauses demanded by the two readings! A very different atmosphere attends an hour when it is the time chosen for a school-girl's escapade or set apart for a poet's meditation. And the voice by its use of pause can preserve or destroy either atmosphere. Try it. Make your pauses in reading the school-girl's text of equal length with the pauses the reading of Lanier's poem demands. You will find the result is that overemphasis which has brought such discredit upon the name of "elocution." I once heard a much-advertised reader strain all the elements of her vocal vocabulary in announcing a simple change in her programme. I have heard more than one reader give the stage directions, indicate the scene setting, and introduce the characters in exactly the same voice and with the same use of emphasis which were afterward employed in the most dramatic passages. Of course all the ammunition had been used up before the real battle began, and no one was in the least affected by the firing during the rest of the engagement.

We have said that the use of pause determines the use of all other elements of the vocabulary. This is particularly true of the change of pitch which immediately follows pause. We pause before a new idea to get possession of it; in that pause we measure the idea, and the pitch of the voice changes to accord with that measure. Every change of thought causes a change of pitch, but the degree and direction of change in pitch of the voice depends upon the degree and direction of change in thought values. In the pause the mind takes time to value the new thought, and tells the voice what change it must make. Robert Browning affords the best material for a study in change of pitch, because of his sudden and long parentheses, which can be handled lucidly by a voice only after it has mastered this element of the vocal vocabulary. Abt Vogler offers the voice an excellent opportunity for exercise in change of pitch. I print the first stanza and first line of the second stanza of this poem for your use.

Would that the structure brave, the manifold music I build, Bidding my organ obey, calling its keys to their work, Claiming each slave of the sound, at a touch, as when Solomon willed Armies of angels that soar, legions of demons that lurk, Man, brute, reptile, fly--alien of end and of aim, Adverse, each from the other heaven-high, hell-deep removed, Should rush into sight at once as he named the ineffable Name, And pile him a palace straight, to pleasure the princess he loved!

Would it might tarry like his, the beautiful building of mine--

Remember, you are to confine your consideration to the one point, change of pitch, not the change of pitch within a word, which is inflection and belongs to another chapter, but to the broad changes of pitch from word to word, phrase to phrase, sentence to sentence, following the intricate changes of the thought.

I leave you to blaze a trail through this forest of ideas. You must find the main road, and then trace the by-paths which lead away from that main road, and in this case, fortunately, come back to it again--which does not always happen in Mr. Browning's "woody tracts of thought." To employ a better figure for vocal purposes, you must cut off the stream, the voice, and trace the bed of this river of thought, following the main channel, and then its branches. You will find the main channel cut by the first and last lines:

Would that the structure brave, the manifold music I build,

* * * * *

Would it might tarry like his, the beautiful building of mine--

All between, beginning with the second line, "Bidding my organ obey," and including the last words of the eighth line, "the princess he loved," is a branch channel, leading away from and coming back to the main river's bed. But this branch channel is interrupted in turn by its own branch leading away from it and returning with it to join the main bed with the last line we quote. This second branch begins in the middle of the third line with the words, "As when Solomon willed," wanders in this course for five lines, and, rejoining the first offshoot, returns to the main channel with the last line. Now turn on the stream, the Voice, and watch it flow into the course as traced. Analyze the reading as to the use of pause and change of pitch.

II

STUDY IN INFLECTION

To me, the most notable among the many notable elements in Madame Alla Nazimova's acting is her illumination of the text of her impersonations through inflection. To an ear unaccustomed to the "broken music" of her speech, a word may now and then be lost because of her still faulty English, but of her attitude toward the thought she is uttering, or the person she is addressing, or the situation she is meeting, there can never be a moment's doubt--so illuminating is the inflectional play of her voice. The tone she uses is not to me pleasing in quality. It does not fall in liquid alluring cadences upon the ear as does Miss Marlowe's, for instance. It is always keyed high, whether the child-wife Nora, or Hedda, omnivorous of experience, is speaking. But this high-pitched tone is endlessly volatile. It is restless. It never lets your attention wander. It is never monotonous. It is a master of inflection. Madame Nazimova's emotion is always primarily intellectual. It always proceeds from a mind keenly alive to the instant's incident. This intensely intellectual temperament reveals itself through her voice in a rare degree of inflectional agility. Recall the revelation of Nora's soul in her cry: "It is not possible! It is not possible!" Madame Nazimova's conception of the mistress of The Doll's House is concentrated in these four words--in her inflection of the last word, I may almost say. When I close my eyes and think of Madame Nazimova's voice I see a grove of soft maples in early October with the sun playing upon them, while Miss Marlowe's tone carries me at once into the pine woods, where a white birch now and then shimmers its yellow leaves. Again, the voice of the Russian actress suggests a handful of diamonds, and the American instrument a set of turquoise in the matrix. The difference in these two agents of two compelling personalities is, of course, the result of a difference in the two temperaments; but undoubtedly it also arises from a difference in methods of training. Whatever the temperament, light and shade can be developed in the voice through practice of inflection; and whatever the temperament, a pure tone can be secured through a mastery of support of breath and freedom of vocal conditions. The voices of these two actresses vividly illustrate these two points. We shall study how to secure Miss Marlowe's tone. We are now to work for Madame Nazimova's light and shade, so far as a mastery of inflection will secure it. How shall we proceed?

"All my life," writes Ellen Terry, in her entrancing memoirs, "the thing which has struck me as wanting on the stage is variety. Some people are tone-deaf, and they find it physically impossible to observe the law of contrasts. But even a physical deficiency can be overcome by that faculty of taking infinite pains." That is the secret of successful acquisition in any direction, is it not-- the faculty of taking infinite pains? With Ellen Terry it resulted in a voice which in its prime estate suggested, it is said, all the riotous colors of all the autumns, or Henry Ward Beecher's most varied collection of precious stones. We can secure an approximate result by employing the same method. Let us proceed with infinite pains to practise, practise, practise inflection.

Let us first examine this change of pitch within a word which we call inflection. How does the pitch change, and why, and what does the change indicate? We have discovered that a change of thought results in a broad change of pitch from word to word, phrase to phrase, sentence to sentence, and we shall discover that a change in emotion results in a change in the color of the tone we are using; but this element of our vocal vocabulary, inflection, is subtler than either of the other two. While change of pitch is an intellectual modulation, and variation in tone-color is an emotional modulation, inflection, in a degree, combines both. It is a change in both color and key within the word. It is primarily of intellectual significance, but it also reveals certain temperamental characteristics which cannot be disassociated with emotion. For instance, the staccato utterance of Mrs. Fiske is technically the result of her use of straight, swift-falling inflections, but it is temperamentally the result of thinking and feeling in terms of Becky Sharp.

Let us see how inflections vary. They rise and fall swiftly or slowly. They move in a straight line from point to point, or make a curve. (The latter we call circumflex inflection.) They make various angles with the original level of pitch, rising or falling abruptly or gradually. These are some of the variations, each indicating an attitude of the mind and heart of the speaker toward the thought, or toward the one spoken to, or toward the circumstances out of which the speech arises. All must be mastered for use at will if light and shade are to be developed in the voice.

Now let us take a phrase or sentence, and voice it under a certain condition, noting the inflection of the word or words which hold the thought of the phrase or sentence in solution. Then let us change the condition and again voice the thought, noting the change in inflection. Let me propound a profound question,--"Do you like growing old?" The answers will all be "yes" or "no." But what of the inflection of those monosyllabic words? Sweet Sixteen will employ a straight, swift-falling inflection on the affirmative (unless some untoward influence, such as "Love the Destroyer," has embittered her life, when she may give us one of May Iverson's adorable replies, masked in indifference and circumlocution). Twenty will employ the straight-falling inflection without the swiftness of Sweet Sixteen's slide. With twenty-five we detect a faint sign of a curve in the more gradual fall. Twenty-eight to thirty-five employs various degrees of circumflex, according to the desire--or possibility--of concealing the real facts. Forty to forty-five, if in defiant mood, employs the abrupt-falling inflection, or, if quite honest, changes to the negative with as swift and straight a fall. This lasts through sixty-five, and at seventy we hear a new and gentle circumflex of the "no," until the pride of extreme old age sets in at eighty-five with the swift fall of sixteen's affirmative. Were it not expedient to maintain friendly relations with one's printer, I should venture to diagram these changes of tone within a word. As it is, I shall content myself with advising you to do so.

It is my privilege to have had acquaintance with a woman who was a personal friend of Emerson. Among the incidents of his delightful talk with her, retold to me, I recall one which bears upon our present problem. They were discussing mutual "Friends on the Shelf." "Have you ever read Titan?" asked the gentle seer. "Yes," replied the lady. "Read it again!" said he. Query to the class: How did the lady inflect the word Yes to call forth the injunction, Read it again? What did her inflection reveal?

However inclined we may be to quarrel with Bernhardt's conception of the Duke of Reichstadt, we can never forget her disclosure of the Eaglet's frail soul through inflection as she crushes letter after letter in her hand and tosses them aside, uttering the simple words, Je d 閨 hire, and the final revelation in the quick, thrilling curve of her wonderful voice on the same words as the little cousin leaves the room at the close of this episode of the letters.

No better material can be chosen for a study of inflection than the paragraph from Emerson's Friendship, quoted in a preceding chapter. Let us repeat the first sentence again. "Our friendships hurry to short and poor conclusions because we have made them a texture of wine and dreams instead of the tough fiber of the human heart." Study, in voicing this, how to illumine the thought by your contrastive inflection of the words "wine and dreams" and "tough fiber of the human heart." A lingering circumflex cadence in uttering the first two words will suggest the unstable nature of a friendship woven out of so frail a fabric as wine and dreams, while a swift, strong, straight-falling inflection on each of the last six words indicates the vigorous growth of a love rooted in the tough fiber of the human heart.

In Monna Vanna Maurice Maeterlinck gives the actress a superb opportunity to show her mastery of inflection. Let us turn to the scene in Prinzivalle's tent:[12]

[12] From Monna Vanna. By Maurice Maeterlinck. Published by Harper & Brothers.

PRINZIVALLE. Are you in pain?

VANNA. No!

PRINZIVALLE. Will you let me have it [her wound] dressed?

VANNA. No! (Pause.)

PRINZIVALLE. You are decided?

VANNA. Yes.

PRINZIVALLE. Need I recall the terms of the--?

VANNA. It is useless--I know them.

PRINZIVALLE. Your lord consents.

VANNA. Yes.

PRINZIVALLE. It is my mind to leave you free....

There is yet time should you desire to renounce....

VANNA. No!

And so the seeming inquisition proceeds. To each relentlessly searching interrogation from Gianello comes Vanna's unfaltering reply, in a single, swift monosyllable, "Yes" or "No." The same word, but, oh, the revelation which may lie in the inflection of that word! Let us try it. Let us read the scene aloud, first giving as nearly as possible the same inflection to each of Vanna's answers, then let us voice it again, putting into the curve of the tone within the narrow space of the two or three lettered monosyllables all the concentrated mental passion of Vanna's soul in its attitude toward the terrible situation and toward the man whom she believes to be her enemy. This is a most difficult exercise, but if "a man's reach should exceed his grasp," it will not retard our progress toward the goal of a vocal vocabulary to attempt it now. Apart from all aim in its pursuit, there is no more fascinating study than this study of inflection. In this day of artistic photography there is an endless interest for the artist of the camera in playing with a subject's expression by varying the light and shade thrown upon the face. So for the student of vocal expression there is endless interest in this play with the thought behind a group of words by varying the inflection of those words. Lady Macbeth's, "We fail!" or Macbeth's, "If it were done when 'tis done, then 'twere well it were done quickly," occurs to us, of course, as rich material for this exercise.

In her analysis of the character of Lady Macbeth Mrs. Jameson gives us an interesting study in inflection, based on Mrs. Siddons's interpretation of the words "We fail." A foot-note reads: "In her impersonation of the part of Lady Macbeth Mrs. Siddons adopted successively three different intonations in giving the words 'we fail.' At first a quick, contemptuous interrogation--'we fail?' Afterward with the note of admiration--'we fail!' and an accent of indignant astonishment laying the principal emphasis on the word we--'we fail!' Lastly, she fixed on what I am convinced is the true reading--'we fail'-- with the simple period, modulating the voice to a deep, low, resolute tone which settled the issue at once, as though she had said: 'If we fail, why then we fail, and all is over.'"

Think how vitally the total impersonation is affected by your choice of inflections at this point. Compare the effects of the three, Mrs. Siddons tested. Are there other possible intonations of the words? What are they? Do you realize the vital effect upon the voice of such vocal analysis and experimentation? Devote ten minutes of the time you take for reading each day to this phase of vocal interpretation, and at the end of a week note its effect upon your silent reading and upon your voice.

Remember, with inflection, as with every other phase of the training, the greatest immediate benefit will come from holding the question of its peculiar significance constantly in mind. Study the temperament of the people about you by noting this element in their speech. Study the attitude of every interlocutor you face, by studying the inflection of his replies to the questions of life and death you propound. But, above all, study your own use of this element. Do not let your own attitude go undetected. It may help you to alter an unfortunate attitude to realize its effect upon your own voice.

STUDY IN TONE-COLOR

And now we must turn to our last point of discussion, tone-color. What is the nature of this element of our vocabulary--this Klangfarbe, this Timbre? Upon what does it depend? You will say, "It is a property of the voice depending upon the form of the vibrations which produce the tone." True! And physiologically the form of the vibrations depends upon the condition of the entire vocal apparatus. Tone-color, then, is a modulation of resonance. But what concerns us is the fact that it is an emotional modulation of resonance. What concerns us is the fact that, as a change of thought instantly registers itself in a change of pitch, so a change of emotion instantly produces a change in the color of the tone--if the voice is a free instrument. And so, as before, I want you not to think of the physiological aspect, but to yield to the emotion, noting the character of the resultant tone, regardless of what has happened in the larynx to produce that result.

As Browning affords us the best material for our study in change of pitch, so the poems of Sidney Lanier offer to the voice the richest field for exercise in tone-color. Musician and poet in one, Lanier's peculiar charm lies in his unerring choice of words, which suggest in their sound, when rightly voiced, the atmosphere of the scene he is painting. Lanier uses words as Corot uses colors. This gives the voice its opportunity to bring out by subtle variations in timbre the variations in light and shade of an atmosphere. To read aloud, sympathetically, once a day, Lanier's The Symphony is the best possible way to develop simultaneously all the elements of a vocal vocabulary. We shall use this poem to-day as a text for our study in tone-color. Let us omit the message of the violins and heavier strings, and take the passage beginning with the interlude upon which the flute-voice breaks:

But presently A velvet flute-note fell down pleasantly Upon the bosom of that harmony, And sailed and sailed incessantly, As if a petal from a wild rose blown Had fluttered down upon that pool of tone And boatwise dropped o' the convex side And floated down the glassy tide And clarified and glorified The solemn spaces where the shadows bide. From the warm concave of that fluted note Somewhat, half song, half odor, forth did float, As if a rose might somehow be a throat; ...

What an ideal for tone-color! Dare we think to make it ours? We must. We must adopt it with confidence of attainment. Let me quote a little further:

When Nature from her far-off glen Flutes her soft messages to men, The flute can say them o'er again; Yea, Nature, singing sweet and lone, Breathes through life's strident polyphone The flute-voice in the world of tone.

Read this passage aloud as a mere statement of fact, employing a matter-of-fact tone. Gray in color, is it not? Now let your voice take the color Lanier has blended for you. Let your tone, like a thing "half song, half odor," float forth on these words and linger as only a perfume can about the thought. Now let the tone change in color to clarify and glorify the following message from the flute:[13]

[13] The extracts on pp. 279-287 are from Mr. Sidney Lanier's volume of "Poems," published by Charles Scribner's Sons.

Sweet friends, Man's love ascends To finer and diviner ends Than man's mere thought e'er comprehends.

I cannot, for lack of space, reprint the whole flute message, but you will get the poem, if you have it not, and voice every word of it, I am sure. Here are some of the most telling lines for our present purpose:

I speak for each no-tongued tree That, spring by spring, doth nobler be, And dumbly and most wistfully His mighty prayerful arms outspreads Above men's oft-unheeding heads, And his big blessing downward sheds. I speak for all-shaped blooms and leaves, Lichens on stones and moss on eaves, Grasses and grains in ranks and sheaves; Broad-fronded ferns and keen-leaved canes, And briery mazes bounding lanes, And marsh-plants, thirsty-cupped for rains, And milky stems and sugary veins; For every long-armed woman-vine That round a piteous tree doth twine; For passionate odors, and divine Pistils, and petals crystalline;

* * * * *

All tree-sounds, rustlings of pine-cones, Wind-sighings, doves' melodious moans, And night's unearthly undertones; All placid lakes and waveless deeps, All cool reposing mountain-steeps, Vale-calms and tranquil lotos-sleeps;-- Yea, all fair forms, and sounds, and lights, And warmths, and mysteries, and mights, Of Nature's utmost depths and heights, --These doth my timid tongue present, Their mouthpiece and leal instrument And servant, all love-eloquent.

You see, to voice this message a mood born of all the "warmths and mysteries and mights of Nature's utmost depths and heights" must take possession of you, and you must yield your instrument to the expression of that mood. Then watch, watch, watch the color of the tone change as the voice, starting with the clear flute-note, follows sympathetically the varying phases of Nature's face which the poet has so sympathetically painted. And now, after a "thrilling calm," the flute yields its place to a sister instrument, and the tone must change its timbre to the reed note of the clarionet. In the "melting" message of that instrument we find two passages which afford the voice chance for a most vivid contrast in color. Beginning with the line, "Now comes a suitor with sharp, prying eye," read the two descriptions which follow, lending your voice to the atmosphere of each:

... Here, you Lady, if you'll sell I'll buy: Come, heart for heart--a trade? What! weeping? why? Shame on such wooer's dapper mercery! I would my lover kneeling at my feet In humble manliness should cry, O sweet! I know not if thy heart my heart will greet: I ask not if thy love my love can meet: Whate'er thy worshipful soft tongue shall say, I'll kiss thine answer, be it yea or nay: I do but know I love thee, and I pray To be thy knight until my dying day.

The first two lines, which set forth a suit in terms of trade, demand a hard, calculating tone, suggestive of large silver dollars. Call this color dull steel gray. This tone flashes out for a moment in the white indignation of the third line, softens and warms with the next two lines, then grows and glows until it reaches a crimson radiance in the last two lines. Try it!

And now, with "heartsome voice of mellow scorn," let us sound the message of the "bold straightforward horn."

"Now comfort thee," said he, "Fair Lady. For God shall right thy grievous wrong, And man shall sing thee a true-love song, Voiced in act his whole life long, Yea, all thy sweet life long, Fair Lady.

Where's he that craftily hath said. The day of chivalry is dead? I'll prove that lie upon his head, Or I will die instead, Fair Lady.

* * * * *

Now by each knight that e'er hath prayed To fight like a man and love like a maid, Since Pembroke's life as Pembroke's blade, I' the scabbard, death was laid, I dare avouch my faith is bright That God doth right and God hath might. Nor time hath changed His hair to white, Nor His dear love to spite, Fair Lady.

I doubt no doubts: I strive, and shrive my clay, And fight my fight in the patient modern way For true love and for thee--ah me! and pray To be thy knight until my dying day, Fair Lady."

Made end that knightly horn, and spurred away, Into the thick of the melodious fray.

Remember your key is set for you,--the color of the tone is plainly chosen for you by Mr. Lanier. Not red nor yellow, but a blending of the two. Orange, is it not? Will not an orange tone give us the feel of heartsome confidence behind and through the mellow scorn of the knight's message? Try it! Let the two primary colors, red and yellow, enter in varying degrees according to, or following, the emotional variation in the thought, as the knight or the lover dominates in the message. In the first seven lines the tone glows with the love radiance and the orange deepens toward red. With the next five lines the lover yields to the knight, and the tone flashes forth a golden, keen-edged sword. With the thirteenth line the tone begins in the orange on "Now by each knight that e'er hath prayed," flashes into yellow in "to fight like a man," softens and deepens toward red in "and love like a maid," and returns to the orange to finish the horn motif.

Next in this poem which affords such a wonderful study for tone-color we have the hautboy's message. The color is mixed and laid on the palette ready for use as before, with the introductory lines:

And then the hautboy played and smiled, And sang like any large-eyed Child,

Cool-hearted and all undefiled.

Don't let the words large-eyed Child mislead you. Don't, I beseech you, make the mistake of adopting the "Little Orphan Annie" tone with which the "elocutionist" too often insults the pure treble of a child's "undefiled" instrument. That is the keynote to us for our choice of color--"cool-hearted and all undefiled." Almost a white tone, is it not? With a little of the blue of the June sky? Try it. Let the blue be visibly present in the first three lines:

"Huge Trade!" he said, "Would thou wouldst lift me on thy head And run where'er my finger led!"

turning to pure white in the next three lines:

Once said a Man--and wise was He-- Never shalt thou the heavens see Save as a little child thou be.

The last voice comes from the "ancient wise bassoons." Again there is danger. Do not, oh! do not fall afoul of the conventional old man's quavering tone. There is nothing conventional about these "weird, gray-beard old harpers sitting on the high sea-dunes," chanting runes. The last words of these introductory lines safeguard us--"chanted runes." There is only one color of tone in which to chant runes. Gray, is it not? Yes, but a silver gray, not the steel gray of the clarionet when she became for the moment a commercial lover. Then in the silver-gray tone of the philosopher, voice this last motif:

Bright-waved gain, gray-waved loss, The sea of all doth lash and toss, One wave forward and one across: But now 'twas trough, now 'tis crest, And worst doth foam and flash to best, And curst to blest.

The importance of a right use of tone-color in vocal interpretation was impressed upon a Browning class last winter. We were reading the Dramatic Lyrics. The poem for the hour was Meeting at Night. The tone with which the first student attacked this exquisite love-lyric was so businesslike, so matter of fact, so utterly out of key, that we who listened saw not the lover hastening to his beloved, but a real-estate agent "out to buy" a farm. The "gray sea, the long black land, the yellow half-moon large and low, the startled little waves that creep in fiery ringlets from their sleep, the pushing prow of the boat quenched in the slushy sand, the warm, sea-scented beach, and the three fields" all assumed a merely commercial value. They were interesting exactly as would be a catalogue of properties in a deed of real estate. If you are not a very intense member of a Browning society you will, I think, enjoy the test of tone-color involved in reading this poem from the contrasted standpoints of the business man and the lover. Of course, in the first instance you must stop where I, in desperation, stopped the student on the words, "a farm appears." For I defy any one to read the last two lines in a gray, matter-of-fact tone.

As was the case in our consideration of inflection, so in this study of tone-color there is an embarrassment of rich material for the exercise of this element. Lanier's Sunrise and Corn; Browning's prologue to The Two Poets of Croisic, with a vivid contrast of color in each verse; Swinburne's almost every line; Dante Gabriel Rossetti, Wordsworth, Keats, Tennyson--but why enumerate? All the colorists among the poets will reward your search of a text for the development of timbre.

For a final brief study of the three elements we aim to acquire, with especial emphasis in thought upon the last one, let us take this prologue to The Two Poets of Croisic, with its color-contrast in each verse:

Such a starved bank of moss Till that May morn, Blue ran the flash across: Violets were born!

Sky--what a scowl of cloud Till, near and far, Ray on ray split the shroud: Splendid, a star!

World--how it walled about Life with disgrace Till God's own smile came out: That was thy face

The vocal treatment of the first two verses will be very much alike. The voice starts in minor key, a gray monotone, in harmony with the absence of color in the bare bank of dull moss. The inflection of the word "starved" must emphasize the grayness. It must be a dull push of the tone on the first syllable, with little, if any, lift above the level of the low pitch on which the whole line is spoken. With a swift, salient, rising inflection on the opening word of the second line, an inflection which creates expectancy of change, the voice lifts the thought out of the minor into the major key. I must call your attention to the vital significance of the use of pause at this point by simply asking you to indulge in it. Stop after uttering the word till and study the effect of the pause. It is the pause quite as much as the inflection, you see, which induces the expectant attitude you desire to create in the mind of your auditor. With the next three words, "that May morn," the tone takes on a bit of the warmth of early summer. A lingering cadence on the word "May" will help the suggestion. With the third line the voice begins to shine. I know no other way to express it. The inflections are swift and straight, but not staccato, because they must suggest a growth, not a burst of color. The tone on which the words are borne must be continuous. It must not be broken off definitely with each word, as is to prove most effective, we shall find, in handling the third line of the second verse. The fourth line brings the full, glowing, radiant tone on the first word, "violets." This tone must be held in full volume on the last two words. The law for beautiful speech must be observed here. (But where should it not be observed?) Let us recall the law, "Beautiful speech depends upon openness of vowels and definiteness of consonants." The vowels give volume to a word, the consonants form. Slur your consonants and squeeze your vowels in the three words of this line, "Violets were born," and what becomes of this miracle of spring? The voicing of the second verse is very like that of the first. The opening line demands the same gray monotone. But the three words, "sky," "scowl," and "cloud," if clear-cut in utterance, as they should be, will break the level of the line more than the single word "starved" in the first line of the first verse can do, or was meant to do. There is the same swift lift of the voice in the opening word of the second line, the same change to the major key, the same growing glow in the tone on the third line, and the same radiant outburst of color sustained through the last line. The only difference lies in the suffusion of radiance in the tone to suggest the coming of color to the bank, in the first verse, and the outburst of radiance to suggest the sudden splitting of the clouds and the star's swift birth, in the second verse. With the emotional change of thought in the last verse, from a travail and birth in nature to a human soul's struggle and rebirth, the deepening color which creeps into the tone indicates the entrance of personal passion. The key does not change. The inflections are still and straight. The tone simply deepens and glows in the last two lines, as a prayerful ecstasy possesses the one who reads.

PART III

STUDIES IN VOCAL TECHNIQUE

THE UNINTERRUPTED TONE

When a rich, dramatic temperament seeks for its instrument of expression the control of faultless technique the result ought to be art of the highest order. Such is the art of Gracia Ricardo. She has translated her English name into musical Italian, but does her country the honor to announce her beautiful voice as an American soprano.

Every tone of Gracia Ricardo's singing voice is as absolutely free from effort as the repeated note of the hermit thrush's song, and her tone as pure tone has the effect of that liquid call. But could you freight the thrush note with knowledge of human passion,--with throb of joy or pulse of pain, you would get from it the effect of Gracia Ricardo's singing of a Heine-Schubert song, a Schumann, Brahms, or Franz lied, or one of our English ballads. It must always be a song, for Gracia Ricardo does not exploit her voice in astonishing vocal feats. She simply sings her song. It was her wish to interpret the lieder of all countries that sent her in search of a method which would free her voice to that high use. She found that method, not in her own country, alas, but in Germany, where for twelve years she has used it in the guidance of her own voice and that of many others. She finds the American pupil "difficult," because "You are so impatient of a long, quiet preparation. You wish to try your skill at every step of the way--and not in the privacy of your study, but in a public's hearing." Poor American public! How it has suffered from this impatience. It is true, is it not, we are not willing to take time to establish a right condition for tone before using the tone in what should be final efforts of the perfected instrument. Blessed be drudgery has not become a beatitude in the gospel of the American artist. When it is so recognized by the student of vocal expression perhaps we can reclaim this great singer and teacher, Madame Ricardo. This book would further that end.

It has been my good fortune while making this book for you to do some brief but intensive studying under Madame Ricardo. It is by her gracious consent that I shall leave with you as an incentive toward the ideal for which we are striving the two watchwords of her teaching which were most potently suggestive to me. The exercises which constitute her method require personal supervision, but the active principle of those exercises for both tone production and breath control is clearly indicated by the two phrases "the uninterrupted tone" and "the constant mouth-breath." These two ideas fully sensed by a voice will work swift wonders in its use.

Like Mr. Mabie's pool of expectancy, these watchwords of the Ricardo method suggest their own application; but let us consider them somewhat more closely. Think then with me of an uninterrupted tone--a tone which is not interfered with at any point in its production. Think of a breath that flows freely on and on, constantly reinforced, but never interrupted--a breath that is allowed to enter the vocal box, pass between the vocal chords, where it is converted into tone; yield itself to the organs of speech and controlled by the speech process, issue from the mouth in beautiful speech forms, in the words which constitute a language!

Tracing the process of tone production in this way, we find that three distinct steps are involved. Even as I write the words distinct and steps I realize their inharmony with the idea of flowing tone. Rather then let us say three phases in the evolution of speech: breath, tone, speech. In using the word speech to designate the final phase in this evolution I am thinking of it in its broadest sense--really in a sense identical with language. With this final phase beyond its mere initiation this book cannot deeply concern itself. For work along this line I must refer you to Prof. T. R. Lounsbury's Standard of Pronunciation in English; to the article on The Acquiring of Clear Speech by John D. Barry, published in Harper's Bazaar for August, September, and October, 1907; to The Technique of Speech, by Dora Duty Jones.

Not technique of speech, but technique of tone is our study. Not how to make beautiful speech forms, but how to make beautiful speech-tones; not how to distinguish one speech from another in a language, or the speech forms of one language from those of another, but how to distinguish interrupted speech-tone from uninterrupted speech-tone--such is our problem.

But tone is breath before it becomes speech, so our first concern is with the initial stage. The process of breath control in the Ricardo method of tone production (as in my own) is analogous to the process of pumping water. Let your chest with its lungs represent the reservoir, your diaphragm, the great muscle at the base of the lungs, becomes the piston and your mouth the mouth of the pump. If the mouth of the pump runs dry the pump itself runs down and has to be primed. Priming a pump is precisely analogous to "catching your breath" in speech.

The active principle of breath control in the Ricardo method is the idea of a constant mouth-breath. A sense of uninterrupted breath is as essential to a knowledge of correct tone as a sense of uninterrupted tone is to a knowledge of correct speech and song.

In breathing to speak or sing there must be such perfect diaphragmatic control that the mouth shall never be out of breath. You must learn in speaking and reading to take easily and quietly breath enough and often enough to supply the tone which is to be made into a single word, a phrase, a sentence, or a series of sentences, and leave the mouth-breath unexhausted, even unaffected. You must never catch your breath; the breath must pass continuously, the mouth-breath remaining a constant quantity.

It was gratifying in my work with this master of tone production to find that my own method in the training of the speaking voice was in accord at almost every point with her method in the training of the singing voice. In reprinting for you the exposition of my own method, as set down in The Speaking Voice, I have found it necessary to make but few changes. I have altered entirely the method of handling the tongue. I have added a word as to the part the lips play in the production of speech. In the few exercises it is safe to offer under the reinforcing of tone I have used the [=e] instead of the ? convinced that it is the more effective vowel sound through which to work for uninterrupted tone.

It was also a pleasure to find my own instrument, through its training for speech, adequately prepared for the work in song. The studies which constitute Part Three of this book, if faithfully attended, will fit your voices for higher work in either art.

LEARNING TO SUPPORT THE TONE

Before attempting the exercises involved in the first step, let us examine a tone in the making, or, rather, let us feel how it is made--for the process of tone production, so far as it concerns us, is not of physiological, but rather psychological, significance. The huge tomes on the physiology of the voice which are of vital interest to the student of anatomy are not only of no use, but are apt to be a positive hindrance to the student of vocal training. A vivid picture of the larynx or vocal cords, a cross-section of the trachea, or a highly illuminated image of any of the cavities concerned in the production of that most wonderful thing in the world, a pure tone of the human voice, is a source of delight to the physiologist, but will only interfere with that feel for the free, full volume of sound which the student of voice as an instrument of thought and emotion is to make, as a first step in vocal training. Then, not as anatomists or physiologists, but as makers of music, let us look at, let us feel for, a tone.

I am "stung by the splendor of a sudden thought"; I desire to share it with you; the desire causes me to take a deep breath, a column of air rises, is converted into tone, passes into the mouth, and is moulded into the words which symbolize my thought. Let us, without further analysis, try this. Close your eyes, think of some line of prose or poetry which has moved you profoundly; let it take possession of you until you are seized by the desire to voice it. Still with closed eyes, feel yourself take the breath which is to be made into tone, and then into the words which stand for the thought. Hold that sensation, and study it with me for a moment. "But," you say, "the desire to voice the thought does not seize me." Very well, let me ask you a question. "Do you believe in examinations?" Now your thought was converted so swiftly into speech that you had no time to study the conversion. Once more, whether your answer be Yes or No, close your eyes and feel for the tone you are to use in making the single word.

Now, a little more in detail, let us see what happens. A thought full of emotion meets the question, the desire to answer is born; the need of breath to meet the desire contracts the diaphragm (the pump); the chest (the reservoir) fills; a column of air, pumped and controlled by the diaphragm, and reinforced in the chest, rises, strikes the vocal cords (the "strings" of the instrument), the strings vibrate, converting the air into sound, into tone; the tone, reinforced in all the chambers of the head, passes into the mouth, and is there moulded by the juxtaposition of the organs of speech (lips, teeth, tongue) into the word, the single, monosyllabic word, Yes or No, which frames the thought. Now, once more, with closed eyes, sense the process and hold the sensation, but do not speak the word. Now, still once more, and this time, speak. Alas! did we say we were "makers of music"? Is this harmony,--this harsh, hard, breathy, strident note? What is the trouble?

First of all, fundamental to all, and beyond a doubt the secret of the dissonance, you did not breathe before you spoke or as you spoke. I mean, really breathe. And that is the first point to be attacked. Breathe, breathe, breathe! you must learn how to breathe; you must get your pump, your diaphragm, into working order, you must master it, you must control it, you must not fetter it, you must give it a free chance to do its work. If you are a man, you have probably at least been fair in not tying down your pump; you have not incased yourself in steel bands and drawn them so tight that your diaphragm could not descend and perform its office. Yes, and if you are the athletic girl of to-day, you have probably learned the delight and benefit of free muscular action. But you may still be suffering from the effect of your mother's crime in this direction. It may have sent you into the world with weakened muscles in control of the great pumping-station upon which must depend the beauty of your voice.

But whatever the condition or the cause, it must, if wrong, be made right. We must learn to breathe properly, freely, naturally. (Do not confuse naturally and "habitually." In this connection these terms are opposites rather than synonyms.) To breathe naturally we must do away with all constriction. We must choose between the alleged beauty of a disproportionately small waist and the charm of a beautiful and alluring voice. We cannot have both. Then, off with tight corsets! Thank Heaven! they are the exception and not the rule to-day. Please note that I distinctly do not say, "Off with corsets," but only "Off with ill-fitting corsets," for which tight is but another name. I believe, to digress a moment, with our present method of dress, a properly fitted corset is an absolute necessity, except in the rare instances where a perfectly proportioned and slender figure is also under the control of firm, well-trained muscles. In a first flush of rapture over the vision of the gentle ladies of Mr. Howell's Altruria, seen Through the Eye of the Needle, we feel that we can take a step toward that paradise by discarding the strait-laced tailored torture the present-day costume prescribes, for the corsetless grace of the Altrurian garment; but our enthusiasm is short-lived, as we realize that we are in modern America and must make as inconspicuously gracious an appearance as possible without violating the conventions. So, as I say, do not discard the corset, which is, for the majority of women, the saving grace of the present fashion in dress; only see that your corset brings out what is best in the figure God gave you, instead of disfiguring it, as undue constriction of any part of your body will inevitably do. Incidentally, by this precaution, save your voice as well.

But until we can be refitted, or readjust the corsets we already wear, and the gowns made over them, we must avoid the discouraging effect of trying to work against the odds of a costume which interferes with our breathing, by making a practice of taking the breathing exercises involved in the first step, at night and in the morning. Five minutes of deep, free breathing from the diaphragm, lying flat on your back in bed at night and before you rise in the morning, will accomplish the desired result. The point in lying flat on your back is that in that position alone you can be sure you are breathing naturally, which is diaphragmatically. Indeed, you cannot, without great effort, and sometimes not even then, breathe any other way than naturally. I cannot tell you why. I can only say, try it and see.

Our first exercise, then, is to lie flat on the back at night and in the morning, when you are perfectly free, and, with closed eyes, take deep, long breaths, letting them go slowly, and studying the accompanying sensation until it is fixed fast and you feel you cannot lose it, but can reproduce, under any condition, the action which resulted in that sensation. The incidental effect of this exercise is to make one very sleepy. Indeed, nothing will so quickly and effectually put to flight that foe of the society woman and business man of to-day, insomnia, as the practice of deep, regular natural breathing. Add counting each respiration, and it is an almost unfailing remedy. The only trouble for our purpose is that it is sometimes so swiftly soporific that we are asleep before the sensation is fixed fast and noted in consciousness: which is one object of the exercise. However, should we find the prescribed five minutes at night interfered with by coming drowsiness, we may yield in sleepy content, "sustained and soothed" by the thought that we shall be in splendid shape for the morning practice, with which nothing must interfere, "not headache, or sciatica, or leprosy, or thunder-stroke."

We are ready now for the third exercise. When, for five minutes in the morning, lying flat on your back, with closed eyes, you have taken deep, long breaths, letting them go slowly, yielding your whole body to the act of respiration, noting the effect and fixing fast the sensation, as a next step you are to stand up and repeat the operation. Still holding the sensation (not by tightening your muscles, or clenching your fists, or setting your teeth, but simply by thinking the sensation, letting it possess you), in this attitude of mind breathe naturally, standing instead of lying down. That is all. Don't be discouraged if the test prove unsatisfactory at first. Try an intermediate step. Sit on the side of your bed, or in a straight-back chair, and, closing your eyes and relaxing all your muscles except those governing the diaphragm, breathe. Now stand, well poised. By well poised, of course, you know I mean with the weight perfectly balanced about the center of gravity, which, in turn, means that a perpendicular dropped from the highest point of the lifted chest without encountering any part of your body, and especially not your abdomen (which should be held always back, so that it is flat, if not actually concave) will fall unobstructed to the floor, striking a point just between the balls of your feet. Standing thus, well poised, place the right hand on your body, just below your ribs at the base of the lungs, and your left hand on your back, just opposite your right hand; then breathe, and feel the diaphragm, as it descends, cause the torso, in turn, to expand from front to back, pressing against either hand. Let the breath go slowly, controlling its emission by controlling the diaphragm.

So the three exercises stand progressively thus:

First.--Breathe naturally, which is diaphragmatically, five minutes at night. (At first you can be sure of doing this only by lying flat on your back.)

Second.--Breathe naturally, which is diaphragmatically, for five minutes in the morning, and note the sensation.

Third.--Stand and test your newly acquired power by trying to breathe diaphragmatically while on your feet.

These three exercises constitute the first step in the first stage of vocal training, and that step is called Learning to Support the Tone.

I know a little girl who, in the beginning of her career, alarmed her parents by refusing to utter a syllable or the semblance of a syllable until she was three years old, when she evidently considered herself ready for her maiden effort at speech. Prepared she proved, for, sitting at the window in her high-chair one day, watching people pass, she remarked quietly and with perfect precision, "There goes Mrs. Tibbets." I find myself secretly wishing it were possible for you to refrain from speech, not for three years, but for three weeks, while you quietly prepare for speech by practising these three breathing exercises. It is quite the customary thing (or ought to be) for the teacher of voice as an instrument of song to require of the student a period of silence--that is, a period in which only exercises are allowed, and songs, even the simplest, are forbidden. However, our only way to secure this condition would be to go into retreat; but, after all, one of the most encouraging things about this work is the remarkable effect upon the speaking voice of simply holding the thought of the right condition for tone, thinking the three exercises I have given you. It is not so remarkable, perhaps, in the light of the experiment recently made (I am told) in one of our great colleges, when three men daily performed a certain exercise, and three other men simply thought it intensely, and the resultant effect upon the muscles used in the act was marvelously similar. I am half afraid to have recalled this, lest you take advantage of the suggestion and relax your effort, or, out of curiosity, make the experiment. Please don't. I offer it only as an incentive to you, to think at least of the desired condition, if you cannot every day indulge in an active effort to attain it.

Please test at once the immediate effect of this third exercise. Take the attitude I have defined, and try once more any full-voweled syllable. I think you will find the tone already improved.

LEARNING TO FREE THE TONE

We have worked, so far, for support of tone. We must now free the supported tone, by freeing the channel for the emission of the breath as it is converted into tone and moulded into speech. We shall find that in learning to support the tone we have gone far toward securing that freedom; but the habit of years is not easily overcome, and every time you have spoken without proper support of breath you have forced the tone from the throat, by tightening the muscles and closing the channel, thus making conditions which must now be reformed by steady, patient effort. Yet it is not effort I want from you now; it is lack of effort. It is passivity; it is surrender. I want you to relax all the muscles which govern the organs concerned in converting the breath into tone and moulding the tone into speech, all the muscles controlling the throat and mouth, including the lips and jaw. I want utter passivity of the parts from the point where the column of breath strikes the vocal cords to where, as tone, it is moulded into the word "No." Surrender to the desire to utter that word. Concentrate your thought on two things: the taking of the breath and the word it is to become. Now, lying down, or sitting easily, lazily, in a comfortable chair, or standing leaning against the wall, with closed eyes, surrender to the thought "No," and, taking a breath, speak. Still hard and unmusical you find? Yes, but I am sure not so hopelessly hard as before. What shall we do to relax the tense muscles, to release the throat and free the channel? At the risk of being written down a propagandist, in the ranks of the extreme dress-reformers, I shall say, first of all, take off those high, tight collars. Again, as with the corset, it is a case of a misfit rather than too tight a fit. If your collar is cut to fit, it need not be too high nor too tight for comfort, and it will still be becoming. You want it to cling to the neck and keep the line. Cut it to fit, and it will keep the line; then put in pieces of whalebone, if necessary, or resort to some of the many other devices now in vogue for keeping the soft collar erect, but don't choke yourself, either by fastening it too tight or cutting it too high. But how simple it would be if we could relax the tension by doffing our ill-fitting corsets and collars. Alas! the trouble is deeper seated than that.

It is an indisputable and most unfortunate fact that nervous tension registers itself more easily in the muscles about the mouth and throat than anywhere else. So, if we live as do even the children of to-day, under excitement, and so in a state of nervous tension, the habit of speaking with the channel only half open is quickly formed, and the voice becomes shrill and harsh. You have noticed that the more emphatic one grows in argument the higher and harder the voice becomes, and, incidentally, the less convincing the argument. This is true of all excitement; the nervous tension accompanying it constricts the throat, and the result is a closed channel. To learn instinctively to refer this tension for registration not to the throat, but to the diaphragm, is a part of vocal training. This can be easily accomplished with children, and the habit established of taking a deep breath under the influence of any emotion. This breath will cause the throat to open instead of shut, and the tone to grow full, deep, and round, instead of high and harsh. The full, deep, round tone will carry twice as far as the high, harsh, breathy one. The one deep breath resulting in the full, deep tone may--nay, will--often serve the same purpose as Tattycoram's "Count five-and-twenty," and save the angry retort.

It is useless to regret, on either ethical or aesthetic grounds, that we were not taught in childhood to take the deep breath and make the deep tone. But let us look to it that the voices and dispositions of our children are not allowed to suffer. Meanwhile, in correcting the fault in the use of our own instruments, we shall go far toward establishing the proper condition with the next generation, since the child is so mimetic that, to hear sweet, quiet, low tones about him will have more effect than much technical training in keeping his voice free and musical. In the same way, the child who hears good English spoken at home seems less dependent upon text-books in grammar and rhetoric to perfect his verbal expression than the child who is not so fortunate in this respect.

To insure the registration of nervous tension in the muscles controlling the diaphragm and not the throat--that is, to form the habit of breathing deeply when speaking under the influence of emotion, is our problem. The present fault in registration will be found to be different with each one of us, or, at least, will cause us "to flock together" according to the place of registration. Each must locate for himself his own difficulty, or go to a vocal specialist and have it located. The tension may be altogether in the muscles governing the throat, or it may be in those about the mouth. There is the resultant, breathy tone, the hard tone, the nasal tone, the guttural tone, the tone that issues from a set jaw or an unruly tongue. All mean tension of muscles somewhere, and must be met by relaxation of these muscles and the freeing of the channel. How to relax the throat shall be our initial point of attack. A suggestion made by my first teacher proved most helpful to me, a suggestion so simple that I did not for the moment take it seriously. "Think," she said, "how your throat feels just before you yawn." "Yes," I replied, irrelevantly, "and just after you have eaten a peppermint--that cool, delicious, open sensation." This impressed her as significant, but not so effective as her suggestion to me, which I felt to be true when I began to think of it seriously, and so, of course, to yawn furiously. Try it.

Think of the yawn. Close your eyes and feel how the deep breath with which the yawn begins (the need of which, indeed, caused it) opens the throat, relaxing all the muscles. Now, instead of yawning, speak. The result will be a good tone, simply because the condition for tone was right. The moment the yawn actually arrives, the condition is lost, the throat closes; but in that moment before the break into the yawn, the muscles about the throat relax and the channel opens, as the muscles controlling the diaphragm tighten and the deep breath is taken.

These, then, are the first exercises in the second step in vocal training. This step is called Freeing the Tone.

First.--Yawn, noting the sensation.

Second.--Just before the throat breaks into the yawn, stop, and, instead of carrying out the yawn, speak. Repeat this fifty times a day, or ten times, as often as you will. Only, keep at it. Take always a single full-voweled monosyllable; one, or four, or no, or love, or loop, or dove, etc.

We cannot, in a printed consideration, touch more in detail upon individual cases, but must confine ourselves to these simple exercises, which will, in general, be swiftly and effectively remedial.

But we must not stop with the throat, which is but part of the channel involved in the emission of breath as speech. There is the tense jaw to be reckoned with--the jaw set by nervous tension, the jaw which refuses to yield itself to the moulding of the tone into the beautiful open vowel and the clean-cut consonant which make our words so interesting to utter. It is the set jaw which, forcing the tone to squeeze itself out, causes it to sound thin and hard. Again, it is surrender and not effort I want. Just as I should try to secure the relaxation of your arm or hand by asking you to surrender it to me, drop it a dead weight at your side for me to lift as I choose, so now I ask you to surrender your lower jaw to yourself. Let it go.

Drop your head forward, resting your chin on your chest. Then raise your head, but not your chin. Let your mouth fall open. Assume for the moment that mark of the feeble-minded, the idiotic, the dropped-open mouth, just long enough to note the sensation. Place your fingers on either side of your head where the jaws conjoin, and open your mouth quickly and with intention. Note the action under your finger-tips. Now let the mouth fall open, by simply surrendering the lower jaw, and note this time the lack of action under your fingers, at the juncture of the jaws. It is this passive surrender which we must learn to make, if we find, on investigation, that we are speaking through a half-open mouth held fast by a set jaw. The set jaw resists and distorts the mould, and the beauty of the form of the word which flows from the mould is lost; the relaxed jaw yields to the moulding of the perfectly modeled word.

In practising this relaxation there is very little danger of going too far, since the set jaw is the indication of a tense habit of thought, of a high-strung temperament, and this habit of thought will never become, through the practise of an outward mechanical exercise, the slack habit of thought which is evidenced by the loose dropping of words from a too relaxed jaw--a habit which must be met by quite the opposite method of treatment. There are many exercises involved in vocal training which must be directed very carefully for a time before the student can be trusted to practise them alone; so I am confining myself in this, as in every step we take together, to the simple, fundamental, and at the same time perfectly safe ones.

To review those for relaxation of the lower jaw:

First.--Drop the head until the chin rests upon the breast. Raise the head, but not the lower jaw.

Second.--With eyes devoid of intelligence and the mouth dropped open, shake the head until you feel the weight of the lower jaw--until the lower jaw seems to hang loosely from the upper jaw and to be shaken by it, as your hand, when you shake it from the wrist, seems to be commanded by the arm, and to have no volition of its own.

Third.--Test your ability to surrender the jaw by placing your fingers on either side your head in front of the ears at the conjunction of the jaws, and first open your mouth with intention, noting the action; then think the word No, and surrender the jaw to the forming of the word, noting the action or absence of action again.

So much for the set jaw. Ten or fifteen minutes a day--yes, even five minutes a day of actual practice with the constant thought of surrender, will reward you. Try it.

And still the channel is not open. There remains that most unruly member, the tongue. Dora Duty Jones refers all faults of technique in speech to failure in the management of the tongue. Miss Jones bases her entire system upon the three words, "On the tongue," in Hamlet's injunction to the players: speak the speech ... trippingly on the tongue. That this organ plays a vital part in the presentation of speech is not to be questioned; that it is the chief actor may be disputed. But whether the tongue is to play a main or a minor part the training to which Miss Jones would subject it is most interesting, and The Technique of Speech[14] should belong to the library of every student of expression. The only danger of this training lies in that of making the tongue a self-conscious actor. What we require of the tongue is that it shall act as a free agent in modeling the perfect word. Many of the exercises given by Miss Jones can be safely attempted only after the preparatory freeing of the organ has been accomplished, but all of them will eventually repay investigation.

[14] The Technique of Speech, by Dora Duty Jones, published by Harper & Brothers.

Meanwhile the following drill for freeing the tongue ought to develop the agility we desire:

First.--Combine l (which may be called the tongue's pet consonant) with ?and repeat the syllable la with constantly increasing speed to form the following groups: l? ... l?l?l? ... l?l?l? ... l? ... l?.

Second.--Change the accent over the vowel and repeat the exercise until all the sounds of a are exhausted in combination with the l.

Third.--Change the vowel and repeat the exercise until all the vowels have been used in combination with l.

Fourth.--Change the consonant to d, then to t, then n, and repeat the exercise.

Fifth.--Follow these exercises on groups of syllables with work on groups of words of one syllable beginning with l, such as: late, lade, lane, lame; last, lack, lank, lapse, laugh; lean, least, leak, leap, lead, etc.

Remember, we are considering primarily speech-tone and not speech form, and that our aim in the exercise of the tongue is to keep it from interrupting the tone.

And now a word must be said as to the part the lips take in speech. It must be only a word, because here more than at any other point the work needs the careful supervision of a trained ear and trained eyes. Madame Ricardo yields to the lips control of the tongue, as she gives to the diaphragm control of the breath. I think she would make easily on the lips rather than "trippingly on the tongue" the controlling principle in tone and speech. I shall give you but one exercise:

Combine the speech process m with the vowel [=e] and let the tone explode easily on the lips in the repeated syllable, m[=e], m[=e], m[=e].

LEARNING TO REINFORCE THE TONE

And now we turn from the second step in the training to the third and last step--the reinforcing of the supported and freed tone. It is again a freeing process. This time we are to free the cavities now closed against the tone; we are to use the walls of these cavities as sounding-boards for tone, as they were designed to be, so reinforcing the tone and letting it issue a resonant, bell-like note with the carrying power resonance alone can give, instead of the thin, dull, colorless sound which conveys no life to the word into which it is moulded by the organs of speech. How shall we free these cavities? I find myself now impatient of the medium of communication we are using. I want to make the tone for you. I want, for instance, to shut off the nasal cavity and let you hear the resultant nasal note, thin, high, unresonant, which hardly reaches the first member of my audience; then I want you to hear the tone flood into the nasal cavity, and, reinforced there by the vibration from the walls of the cavity, grow a resonant, ringing, bell-like note, which will carry to the farthest corner of the room without the least increase in loudness. But we must be content with the conditions imposed by print.

First, you must realize that so-called "talking through the nose" is not talking through the nose at all, but rather failure to do so--that is, instead of letting the tone flood into the nasal cavity, to be reinforced there by striking against the walls of the cavity, which act as sounding-boards for the tone confined within that cavity, we shut off the cavity, and refuse the tone its natural reinforcement. It takes on, as a result, a thin, unresonant quality which we call nasal, although it is thin and unpleasing because it lacks true nasal resonance. The only remedy lies in ceasing to shut off the cavity. Think the sound [=oo]. Let the tone on which it is to be borne grow slowly in thought, filling, filling, and, as it grows, flooding the whole face. Let it press against your lips (in thought only as yet), feel your nostrils expand, your face grow alive between the eyes and the upper lip, that area so often inanimate, lifeless, even in a mobile, animated countenance. Now let the sound come, but let it follow the thought, flood the face, let the nostrils expand, feel the nasal cavity fill with sound; let it go on up into the head and strike the forehead and the eye-sockets and the walls of all the cavities so unused to the impact of sound, which should never have been shut out. Now begin, with lips closed, a humming note, m-m-m. Let it come flooding into the face, until it presses against the lips, demanding the open mouth. Now let it open the mouth into the e. Repeat this over and over--m-[=e], m-[=e], m-[=e]. Don't let the tone drop back as the mouth opens. Keep it forward behind the upper lip, which it has made full, and which, playing against, it tickles until we must let the tone escape. Just as much of the day as possible, think the tone in a flood into the face, and as often as possible hum and let it escape, noting its increasing resonance. It will increase in resonance, I promise you. It will lose its thin, high-pitched nasal quality, and grow mellow and rich and ringing.

And so, with chest lifted, diaphragm at work, throat open, tongue free, jaws relaxed, and all the cavities concerned in vocalization open to the tone, as you breathe and yawn and hum, let it issue a full, round, resonant, singing note to add itself to the music of the world.

A LAST WORD TO THE PUPIL

Mr. William James tells us that we learn to swim in winter and to skate in summer. The principle underlying this statement is of immense comfort in approaching a class in vocal expression. The hope of satisfying results is fostered by the knowledge that a mere statement of the fundamental facts of right tone production will do much toward inducing a right condition for tone. But I know, too, that immediate results depend upon immediate and faithful putting into practice of the principles set forth. A little practice every day will work swift wonders with the voice. And so, in leaving with you Madame Ricardo's watchwords, I also commend you to Ellen Terry's "infinite pains." When it means, as it does in pursuing this ideal, that we must be on guard every waking instant--for a time; when it means a watch set (for a time) upon every organ involved in expression--lips, teeth, tongue, jaw, mouth, throat, chest, diaphragm, and all the muscles governing these organs; when it means a watch set (for a time) upon one's every thought and emotion lest it make false demands upon the sensitive instruments of their expression--then it becomes a daring device, indeed, to wear upon one's crest. Let us not hesitate to carve it there, when we realize that to follow it means culture, true culture, the culture which can only come through control and command of one's self.

TO THE TEACHER

When I consider how much depends in the training of a voice upon listening to the made tone, how little depends upon knowing how it was made, I realize that it is your ear, not my book, which must become the real guide in this Study of Vocal Expression.

###

www.ingramcontent.com/pod-product-compliance
Lightning Source LLC
Chambersburg PA
CBHW070857180526
45168CB00005B/1856